THE LIFE AND TIMES OF
MARK TWAIN

THE LIFE AND TIMES OF
MARK TWAIN

DENNIS WELLAND

CRESCENT BOOKS
New York

PHOTOGRAPHIC ACKNOWLEDGEMENTS

The publishers would like to thank the following collectors and museums for permission to reproduce the photographs and illustrations in this book. Particular thanks are due to the Mark Twain Memorial, Hartford, Connecticut and also to Nick Karanovich, Indiana.

Mark Twain Memorial, Hartford, Connecticut: 8, 9, 10 (top), 11 (right), 12 (left and bottom), 20 (right), 21 (bottom right), 22, 23, 24 (right), 42 (bottom right), 52 (top), 55 (top left and right), 57, 58 (top), 62 (bottom), 63 (centre and bottom), 64, 67, 68 (top), 70 (right), 71, 72, 77 (right), 116 (bottom), 118, 122 (bottom left), 123 (top), 124, 125, 126 (bottom), 133 (top), 139; The Mansell Collection, London: 16, 30 (bottom), 32 (top right), 41, 80 (right), 88, 97 (bottom), 102, 106 (top), 111 (bottom), 114 (both bottom left), 122 (bottom right), 125 (bottom), 130 (top left), 131 (bottom right), 135 (bottom), 136, back jacket; Peter Newark's American Pictures, Bath: 14 (centre bottom), 18 (bottom), 19 (main picture), 29 (top right, centre right), 50, 53 (bottom), 54, 60 (top), 61 (centre right), 63 (top left), 78 (top), 79 (bottom), 120 (top); Mark Twain Birthplace State Historic Site, Stoutsville, Missouri: 70 (right), 121, 130 (top right); Becky Thatcher Book Shop, Hannibal, Missouri: 11 (top left, right and centre), 24 (left), 56 (top), 84 (bottom), 138 (bottom), 141 (centre right), 143 (bottom right); Stowe-Day Foundation, Hartford, Connecticut: 62 (bottom); The Bridgeman Art Library, London/Reynolds Museum, Winston Salem, North Carolina: 10 (bottom); Bridgeman/Private Collection: 28 (bottom), 36 (bottom); Bridgeman/Fine Art Society, London: 38; Bridgeman/New York Historical Society: 58 (bottom), 66, 73; BFI Stills, Posters and Designs, London: 68 (bottom right), 69 (bottom); BFI/United Artists-Readers Digest: 68 (bottom left), 69 (top), 70 (left); BFI/Universal: 81 (far right), 83 (top), 84 (top), 85 (right), 86 (bottom right), 87 (top right); BFI/20th Century Fox: 104 (bottom left), 105 (top), 106 (bottom), 109 (top); Illustrated London News Picture Library: 112 (bottom right); Robert Harding Picture Library, London: 52; Robert Harding/Yale University: front jacket; Robert Harding/Museum of the City of New York Photo Library: 137; Yale University Art Gallery, Mabel Brady Garvan Collection: 12 (top right); Nick Karanovich (photography Ronald W May): 94 (top), 109 (centre right and bottom), 120 (bottom left), 134, 140, 143; The Mander and Mitchenson Theatre Collection, Beckenham, Kent: 101 (bottom); Martha Swope, Photographer, New York/Lawrence Till Collection: 86; Doug Johnson and Ward Graham Designers, New York/Lawrence Till Collection: 86 (top centre); Southern Pacific R.R.: 17; Brown Bros: 21 (right); Library of Congress, Washington, D.C.: 27 (left); A.J. Russell (American Geographical Society): 34 (bottom); Santa Fe R.R.: 60 (centre right); the New York Public Library (Henry W. and Albert A. Berg Collection, Astor, Lenox and Tilden Foundation)/University of California, Berkeley: 134; J-L Charmet, Paris: 26, 33 (bottom), 39, 41 (bottom), 132 (bottom left and right); Author's collection: 81 (bottom left), 107 (bottom right), 138 (top); Dr. Robert McIntyre: 98 (top); Marlborough Photo Library, Bath: 96 (top); Chatto and Windus London: 122 (top left); Samuel C. Webster: 13; Terra Sancta Arts/Courtesy of the Victoria & Albert Museum Library, London: 44; Robert Opie Collection, Gloucester: 74 (bottom); Bass Export Ltd., Glasgow: 142; South Place Ethical Society, London: 99 (bottom); Surrey Local Studies Library, Guildford: 133 (bottom).

Publisher's Note: The publishers have made every effort to locate and credit the copyright holders of material reproduced in this book, and they apologise for any omissions.

This edition published 1991 by Crescent Books,
distributed by Outlet Book Company, Inc.
A Random House Company
225, Park Avenue South
New York, New York 10003.

First published 1991 by Studio Editions Ltd.
Princess House, 50 Eastcastle Street,
London W1N 7AP, England.

Copyright this edition © Studio Editions Ltd., 1991.

Designed by Watermark Communications Group Ltd.,
Chesham, England.

ISBN 0-517-05918-5

Printed and bound in Czechoslovakia.

8 7 6 5 4 3 2 1

CONTENTS

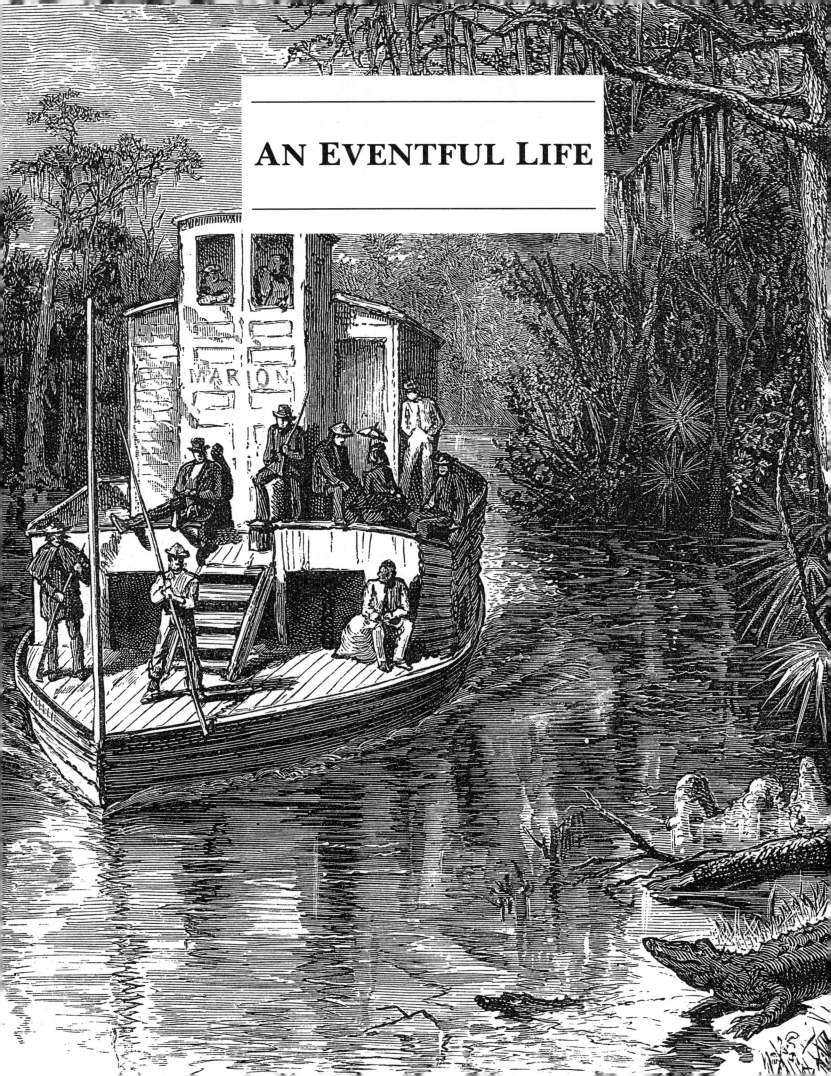

An Eventful Life

AN EVENTFUL LIFE

No American writer's name is better known throughout the world than Mark Twain's, though there are many with whose writings the modern reader will have a wider and closer familiarity. His fame as an American humorist has made into near-proverbs many sayings attributed, not always correctly, to him. These are quoted, or misquoted, by journalists, broadcasters and after-dinner speakers the world over, few of whom, probably, would have read (or perhaps could even name) many of his books beyond *The Adventures of Tom Sawyer* and *The Adventures of Huckleberry Finn*. To those who think of him only as a children's author, the full range and diversity of his prolific output would come as a genuine surprise. Yet in his lifetime more than 1,150,000 authorized copies of his books were published in Britain alone, as well as countless cut-price pirate copies; he sold widely and well in Europe, especially in translation, and the number published in North America (even excluding pirate copies) is incalculable.

When Mark Twain was fifty, he told a correspondent: "Yes, the truth is, my books are simply autobiographies. If the incidents were dated, they could be strung together in their due order, and the result would be an autobiography." This is true, of course, only as long as it is not taken too literally. As with any work of art, allowance must be made for the way in which the remembered past is transmuted by the creative imagination, and Mark Twain's imagination was unusually fertile in its creativity.

Late in life, at intervals and quite unsystematically, he dictated his reminiscences. From these incomplete, and seldom verifiable, recollections his secretary, Albert Bigelow Paine, and others have constructed a reasonably coherent and very readable *Autobiography*, but three things have to be kept in mind before trusting that book too far. First, Mark Twain's dictations were for his own amusement rather than for publication, and thus one can seldom be sure how far it is his imagination rather than his memory that is at work. Second, he once remarked on his own ability to remember only those things that had never happened.

TWAIN IN OXFORD *(1908) (opposite), after being awarded the degree of Doctor of Literature. He continued to wear the scarlet and grey robe with great pride from then on.*

MARK TWAIN IN 1902 *(below), standing outside his birthplace home, a log-wood cabin, in Florida, Missouri.*

TWAIN THE SMOKER, *1907 (right): "I had been a smoker from my ninth year" (Autobiography). Although his wife disapproved, Twain continued to enjoy his cigars, his only rule being "never to smoke more than one at a time".*

YELLOWSTONE GRAND CANYON *(below), by Thomas Moran (1837–1926). An Englishman, born in Bolton, Lancashire, Moran became one of the major painters who depicted authoritatively the American West. Twain shared Moran's response to the grandeur of such scenery dwarfing human activity.*

Third, for a variety of reasons, not necessarily reprehensible, editors must, by definition, use their discretion as to what they include and what they omit. Yet, even with these reservations, this *Autobiography* must inevitably be frequently drawn on in a book such as this, and therefore, in the text that follows, first-person statements, in quotation marks and not otherwise identified, may be taken as coming from it.

The present account of his life, his writings and his world is organized on geographical rather than on strictly chronological lines. The two synchronize better than might be expected, but the intention is to stress the importance of travel in his work as well as in his life. Few of his contemporaries had so strong a claim to be called men of the world in the most literal meaning of the phrase, but he had also the happy knack of being able to highlight, wherever he was, things of interest and relevance to the still relatively young United States.

In those days, of course, long before the advent of inexpensive photography, travel films and documentaries, and when travel itself, even within the continental United States, was tedious, hazardous and costly, people turned avidly to books and pictures for information about the world in which they lived. However, the standard of colour printing available to the general public even in the lithographs of the famous firm of

Currier & Ives was often more reliable than the accuracy of the scene depicted. The American landscape was also already a source of fascination to many important American painters. Several of them had, as official artists, accompanied survey parties opening up the new American West, but their first-hand knowledge of their subjects was accessible to the contemporary public only through the less-than-satisfactory medium of uncoloured line engravings in books and newspapers, often made worse by the inferior quality of the paper on which they were reproduced. The printed word was indispensable to reinforce images.

The work of many American writers and artists has always been firmly grounded in the region of their birth, but the range of Mark Twain's travels and experience makes it impossible to categorize him neatly as a regionalist. Born and raised in the Old South, he was nearing his fifties before he produced the works most directly inspired by that region. Although he was almost thirty-four before he published his first full-length book, his contemporaries came to look to him for information about the American West, about life on the Eastern seaboard, even about Europe and the Holy Land, before thinking of him as a product of the American South.

Like many humorists, Mark Twain had literary aspirations beyond mere entertainment. Like others, he found that this could create difficulties for some readers. On a train between Liverpool and London in 1872 he was delighted to observe the passenger opposite reading *The Innocents Abroad* during the entire journey of almost five hours. The author's pleasure diminished when not a single smile appeared in that time. The passenger may even have been the unidentified Lancashire hatter

whose copy of the second volume of the book is now in my possession: he took it so seriously as to adorn the margins either by sidelining factual and statistical information for future reference or by scribbling pencilled comments. Most of these are protestations of outrage, such as "Mark, you don't read your Bible!" or sometimes "Rubbish!" against a passage vigorously crossed out. Mark Twain seems to have won him over eventually, though, for at the end he notes approvingly "Well written, Mark!"

Even Mark Twain's own attitude to the professional humorist was equivocal. Towards the end of his life, looking back on an anthology he had published in 1888 as *Mark Twain's Library of Humor*, he declared "This book is a cemetery". The writers it included were forgotten "because they were merely humorists. Humorists of the 'mere' sort cannot survive. Humor is only a fragrance,

COUNTRY SCHOOL (top right), by
E. L. Henry N.A., 1890. Twain
went to three different schools in
Hannibal, but the part of his
education that he "looked back
upon with most satisfaction" was
the country schoolhouse three
miles from his uncle's farm which
he attended "with more or less
regularity once or twice a week,
in summer" (Autobiography).

PRINTER'S DEVIL (right). When
his father died in 1847, Twain
was forced to leave school to help
support the family. He began
work as an apprentice printer on
the Hannibal Courier, then
went on to work for his brother
Orion on the Journal, "where I
served in all capacities, including
staff work" (Autobiography).

a decoration." When he goes on to say "I have always preached. That is the reason that I have lasted thirty years", his tongue is not entirely in his cheek. On the other hand, he would not have concurred happily with the conclusion, drawn from this statement by some solemn Russian enthusiasts, that his work must be read primarily as social criticism lightly garnished with occasional touches of humour.

The desire to inform, educate and stimulate his reader on serious issues became stronger as popularity led Mark Twain to realize his potential influence and the size of his readership. Social criticism is certainly an important element, and he took sides vigorously in many issues of international importance, devoting to the activity rather more time and energy than was good for his enduring reputation. His opinions on such matters were frequently more partisan than original and he easily became over-earnest in his didacticism. Ironically, the books for which he hoped and expected to remain famous are today unknown to most readers except the specialists. What remains impressive is that a talent so diverse and influential should have come from such unpromising beginnings.

Samuel Langhorne Clemens was born on "the 30th November, 1835, in the almost invisible village of Florida, Monroe County, Missouri . . . The village contained a hundred people and I increased the population by one per cent. It is more than many of the best men in history could have done for a town." He also boasted that his arrival in the world coincided with one of the arrivals of

Halley's Comet. Though the family was not rich, his father employed slaves: "I had no aversion to slavery. I was not aware that there was anything wrong about it." Not until he was four did the family move to Hannibal, the little hamlet on the Mississippi (sometimes wrongly thought of as his birthplace) that was to be the setting for the adventures of Tom Sawyer and Huckleberry Finn. But "Mark Twain", their creator, was not born until the 1860s. It is important to separate the man from the persona he deliberately adopted as an author, though the complex relationship between them must be borne in mind to understand him fully.

Like many of us, he remembered his school-days with mixed feelings. The happiest of them, which he immortalized by recreating them half a century later in heightened form in *Tom Sawyer* and *Huckleberry Finn*, will be discussed in the context of those two works, but some of the liveliest passages in the *Autobiography* towards the end of his life are still the affectionate vignettes of his childhood companions. However, being ridiculed for his inability to chew tobacco by "a strapping girl of fifteen, in the customary sunbonnet and calico dress", humiliated him: "I determined to reform. But I only made myself sick; I was not able to learn to chew tobacco. I learned to smoke fairly well but that did not conciliate anybody and I remained a poor thing and characterless . . . Children have but little charity for one another's defects." Such experiences were to lead him to the wider realization he attributes to Huck: "Human beings can be awful cruel to one another." Nevertheless, Clemens's dedication to smoking was lifelong, and Mark Twain deliberately cultivated it as one of his trademarks.

His parents had married in their twenties in Lexington, Kentucky, in 1823: "Neither of them had an overplus of property." Samuel was their fifth child. His mother he remembered particularly because "She never used large words but she had a natural gift for making small ones do effective work. She lived to reach the neighborhood of ninety years and was capable with her tongue to the last — especially when a meanness or an injustice roused her spirit . . . Her interest in people and other animals

was warm, personal, friendly. She always found something to excuse, and as a rule to love, in the toughest of them — even if she had to put it there herself." These were characteristics he inherited from her in full measure and used in his writings.

The senior Clemenses originally established themselves in Jamestown, Tennessee, where John Clemens became the owner of a large tract of land. Here their first four children, Orion, Pamela, Margaret and Benjamin, were born. "I was postponed —", Samuel claimed, "postponed to Missouri. Missouri was an unknown new state and needed attractions." In fact it was heavy losses in the financial crash of 1834 that constrained John Clemens to move himself and his family to Florida, Missouri. "He

FOUR GENERATIONS OF TWAIN'S FAMILY *(below), photographed in New York on the occasion of his mother's seventy-ninth birthday in 1882. Seated are Jane Clemens (left) and Twain's sister Pamela Clemens Moffett (right), with Pamela's daughter Annie Moffett Webster standing behind, and her daughter Jean in front with her doll.*

'kept store' there several years but had no luck, except that I was born to him." After Samuel there was also a sixth child, Henry. Even after the subsequent move to Hannibal, disaster still dogged John and he died, in 1847, in his forties. His son, almost twelve at the time, was to recall that he had never seen or heard him laugh, but even more painfully vivid throughout his life was the memory of having watched through a keyhole the autopsy being carried out on his father's body.

"The Clemens family was penniless again." This meant the early end of schooling for young Samuel and he was apprenticed as a printer to the publisher of the *Courier*. He later left the *Courier* to work in the same capacity for his brother Orion, when, a couple of years later, the latter returned to Hannibal as proprietor of the *Journal*. Sam occasionally contributed short

pieces himself: "My literature attracted the town's attention 'but not its admiration' (my brother's testimony)." The early failure of the *Journal* cannot have been attributable to this alone. Orion, luckless as his father and forced to economize, "moved the whole plant into the house we lived in, and it cramped the dwelling place cruelly."

This most literally "in house" activity also failed in its turn, and Orion eventually

disposed of the paper and left Hannibal. Sam went independently to St Louis. "There I worked in the composing room of the *Evening News* for some time and then started on my travels to see the world." These took him, still as a printer, to New York and Philadelphia, a distance not inconsiderable in those days but minuscule in comparison with his later journeys. Disillusioned, he rejoined Orion, who had acquired a printing plant in another small Missouri town. "I worked in that little job office in Keokuk as much as two years, I should say, without ever collecting a cent of wages, for Orion was never able to pay anything."

Printing was a trade which an earlier American writer, also of humble origins, Benjamin Franklin, had followed with exemplary industry, but Mark Twain was never an admirer of the virtues Franklin advocated. Nevertheless, he must have practised the thrift that Franklin extolled, for by 1857, despite Orion's inadequacies as an employer, Sam had somehow accumulated enough money to afford a passage down the Mississippi by riverboat to New Orleans.

He had read a book by an explorer of South America and "been mightily attracted by what he said of coca". Franklin would have approved whole-heartedly of his successor's enterprise and his aim: "I made up my mind that I would go to the headwaters of the Amazon and collect coca and trade in it and make my fortune."

The meticulous Franklin, however, would not have neglected the precaution of preliminary enquiries. Characteristically, Sam Clemens delayed until his arrival in New Orleans, where "I inquired about ships leaving for Para and discovered that there weren't any and learned that there probably wouldn't be any during that century." Penniless once more in the true family tradition, he decided that his best option was to fulfil a childhood ambition by apprenticing himself to a riverboat captain as a Mississippi pilot.

His four years on the river formed the period of his life on which he looked back with most affection and nostalgia, and which, as will be seen from Chapter 4, was later to produce much of his most memorable writing. Yet, ironically, had he been

able to continue in contented obscurity piloting steamboats up and down the river he had loved since childhood, his literary career might have ended there before it had properly begun. Already the incursive railroad was destined gradually to supersede the old paddle-steamers as a mode of

STREET SCENE IN PHILADELPHIA *(above), late nineteenth century. From New York Twain moved to Philadelphia, where he worked as a "sub" on the* Inquirer *and the* Public Ledger.

"FLATBOATMEN ON THE MISSISSIPPI" *(left), by Charles Wimar (1828–1862). Finding that his plans to make a fortune from trading in coca in the Amazon were thwarted, Twain persuaded the Mississippi pilot, Horace Bixby, to take him on as a cub.*

COTTON STEAMER *(below) of the kind that carried freight along the Mississippi.*

PILOT-HOUSE (*above*). "*When I stood in her pilot-house I was so far above the water that I seemed perched on a mountain*" (Life on the Mississippi).

written for the New Orleans press and ridiculed by one "Sargeant Fathom" who may have been Clemens himself. Later, after using "Josh" for a while, and learning that Captain Sellers was dead, he appropriated the pseudonym, confident that Sellers had no longer any use for it. Whatever the truth of its origin, the name came from the river and was peculiarly appropriate for its illustrious user.

The leadsmen on the riverboats, taking soundings in fathoms on the more treacherous parts of the river, would call them in the form "By the mark four!" or "Mark three-and-a-half!" The critical level of water, below which the boat would be in danger of running aground, was two fathoms,

transport, but the inevitable decay of river traffic was to be prematurely accelerated by an event far more disastrous: the outbreak in 1861 of what the South came to know as the "War between the States".

When he did resume his literary career, an author looking for a pseudonym, he chose one from the river. To be specific, he borrowed one which, according to Clemens, a certain Captain Sellers had used as a pen-name for short pieces on river traffic

NEW ORLEANS MARKET (*right above*). *The stretch of the Mississippi that Twain learned from Bixby covered the 1,200 or so miles of bends and bars from St. Louis to New Orleans.*

LOADING COTTON ON THE MISSISSIPPI (*right*), *lithograph by Currier and Ives, c. 1850. With the outbreak of the Civil War, river commerce was suspended and Twain had to look for a new job.*

16

THE BATTLE OF WILLIAMSBURG, (left), by Louis Kurz. In June 1861 Twain joined the Confederate Army as a second lieutenant in the Marion Rangers but resigned after two weeks' service in the field.

announced urgently as "Mark twain!" There is an appropriateness in that derivation of the pen-name, for until it had earned him such fame that he could use no other he continued to sign "S.L. Clemens" to his more serious work. "Mark Twain" he restricted consistently to journalistic pieces that were deliberate hoaxes, political burlesques or light-hearted accounts of travel: pieces, that is, on the dangerous borderline between the safe water of authenticity and the shallows of that uncertain area in which a reputation may founder through blurring the distinction between verifiable fact and humorous invention. Had it not been for the outbreak of the Civil War, though, "Mark Twain" might have been stillborn.

The imminence of war precipitated him into the career in which he spent the shortest time. He immediately enlisted in the Confederate army. If we can believe the account he gave of it in "The Private History of a Campaign that Failed", his soldiering was brief and inglorious. All it taught him, he says there, was "more about retreating than the man that invented retreating", and, after only one short confrontation with the enemy, he and his companions announced that "the war was a disappoint-

ment to us and we were going to disband". (The *Autobiography* puts it more colourfully: "I resigned after two weeks service in the field, explaining that I was 'incapacitated by fatigue' through persistent retreating.") Or, to use the phrase of Ernest Hemingway's hero in *A Farewell to Arms*, he "made a separate peace" and left, but not before almost meeting the man who was to become

THE GOVERNOR STANDFORD, first locomotive on the Central Pacific Railroad (below). The railroad had yet to be built when Twain travelled west with his brother Orion in 1861.

A FREIGHTERS' CAMP, WEST
VIRGINIA (right). In the pre-
railroad era, all freight travelled
overland on wagons.

GENERAL ULYSSES S. GRANT
(above), leader of the Union
forces. Although Twain fought in
the opposing army during the
Civil War, the two men were to
come much closer later in their
lives.

GENERAL GRANT IN ACTION
(above right), at the Battle of
Shiloh in Tennessee.

PIONEERS HEADING WEST BY
WAGON TRAIN, WITH ROCKY
MOUNTAINS BEHIND (right),
lithograph by Currier and Ives,
1868. To Twain, as to many
settlers in the 1860s, the
American West offered the
promise of a bright future. This
picture idealizes the terrain and
separates by a river benign
Indians from peaceful pioneers to
heighten this promise.

the hero of the war, Ulysses S. Grant.
"I came within a few hours of seeing him
when he was as unknown as I was myself",
says the "Private History", though admit-
ting modestly that at the time young Clemens "was proceeding in the other direction". In the Autobiography this has been
characteristically inflated into "I came near
to having the distinction of being captured
by Colonel Ulysses S. Grant". Whatever the
truth of this incident, the two men were to
come much closer later in their lives.

Clemens's next decision was the one he
was to attribute more than twenty years
later to young Huck Finn: to "light out for
the territory ahead of the rest". "The territory" in nineteenth-century America meant
the vast but diminishing frontier area to the
west of the settled States, the virgin land of
infinite opportunity. In 1861 Nevada was
the territory in process of being settled, and
by a happy coincidence Orion had at last
abandoned newspaper publishing to become Secretary of the Territory of Nevada,
a post which necessitated his deputizing for
the Governor in the latter's absence. Moving thither to take up his new appointment
he took with him, as his own secretary, his
younger brother (who was to claim to have
paid the fares for both of them himself).

PANNING FOR GOLD AT SUTTERS' FORT (left) by Dean Cornwall. The California Gold Rush of 1849 had awakened dreams of instant wealth which Twain shared.

Orion Clemens thereby unwittingly altered Sam's career and the whole course of American literature. This phase of our hero's career, as unheroic as those preceding it, is treated in the next chapter. Dreams of untold quantities of silver and gold were driving prospective miners to Nevada and beyond in their hundreds. After a short and abortive attempt at this, Samuel Clemens proved the West to be a land of opportunity for him by becoming a journalist and, in time, a world-famous popular author.

However, beginning as a journalist, dominated by topicality and a deadline, was not necessarily beneficial to him as a major creative writer whose early facility in writing needed a different sort of control. Indeed, Mark Twain may not unfairly be said to be one of the few indisputably great writers who never produced a book that is consistently great throughout. Even in his lifetime his colourful personality distracted attention from his literary ability at its best, popular though it made him as a lecturer, raconteur and entertainer.

His impulsive iconoclasm, while in the highest degree amusing, led to the lapses of taste which worried the literary establishment of the Eastern seaboard (including his great friend William Dean Howells, novel-

AN EMIGRANT WAGON (above) was a familiar sight in the new territories.

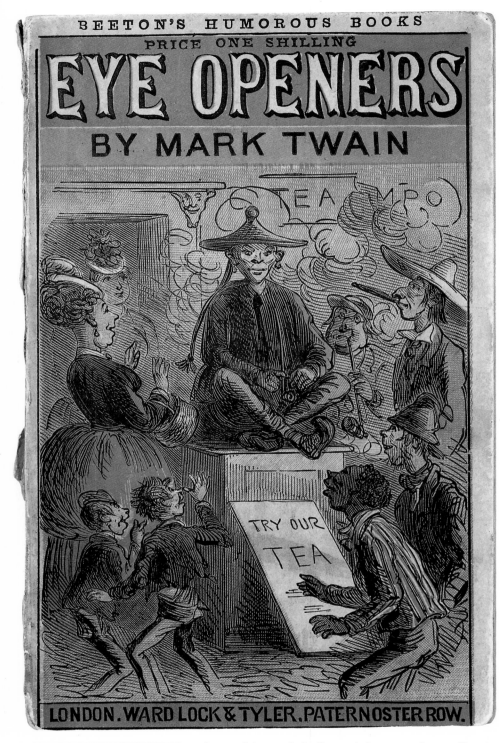

BEETON'S HUMOROUS BOOKS

PRICE ONE SHILLING

EYE OPENERS
BY MARK TWAIN

TEA

TRY OUR TEA

LONDON. WARD LOCK & TYLER. PATERNOSTER ROW.

JACKET OF MARK TWAIN'S *EYE OPENERS* (above), an English piracy. Twain's early humorous pieces were published in collections on both sides of the Atlantic.

Initially his humorous pieces were slight sketches published either in the popular press or in cheap paperback collections. There was at that time an enormous vogue for this kind of writing in the United States, and naturally British visitors brought specimens home with them. As there was effectively no enforceable law of International Copyright until 1891, these were promptly and unscrupulously pirated by a number of publishers and retailed profitably on railway station bookstalls. Mark Twain quickly became lucrative to the pirates, who frequently, to enlarge the book somewhat, would attribute to him pieces by other American writers. Some of them were not above commissioning pastiche pieces specially concocted by their own hacks, much to the indignation of the original author.

Slight as they are, these early pieces helped him to form the literary style which made him famous. He transfers to the printed page a version of the vernacular idiom of everyday common life, losing none of its raciness while often investing it with an imaginative intensity and eloquence far beyond its surface meaning. These pieces

ist, critic and influential magazine editor) and irritated even more his own long-suffering, if somewhat over-proper, wife Olivia. The liveliness of his mind, the range of his interests, and the mercurial nature of his temperament, even more than his lack of any formal education and a chronic disposition to indolence, created the inability to concentrate and the tendency to digress which, amusing though it often is, can also lead to unevenness in his writing.

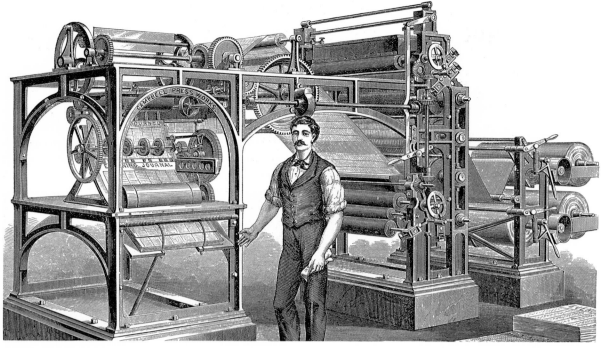

AMERICAN PUBLISHING
COMPANY ADVERTISEMENT
(*opposite, bottom*). *By 1869, the
year that* The Innocents
Abroad *was published, Twain
had already established a
considerable reputation.*

NINETEENTH-CENTURY
NEWSPAPER PRINTING (*left*).
*When silver-mining failed him,
Twain began work as a journalist
on the Virginia City* Enterprise.

quickly ensured for him a ready audience for the full-length books to which he soon turned. With these and their successors he was to keep readers across the world entranced over a period of forty years, earning for himself, and losing, a substantial fortune in the process, making many friends, and travelling thousands of miles.

Yet there was to be a dark side to this, and he was not the first humorist to find that amusing other people was no guarantee against personal unhappiness and tragedy. When he died on 21 April 1910, honoured and loved as he was by then, he was in many

ways still the "Innocent Abroad" of his first book or the simple country boy he immortalized as Huckleberry Finn, alternately fascinated and repelled by the strange wonder of a wide and constantly changing world in which he was never totally at home.

From experiences like being made to feel "a poor thing and characterless" over his failure to chew tobacco, he had accumulated since childhood a steadily increasing burden of guilt, though not always with justification. With what strength of personal feeling he must have written Huck's words: "It don't make no difference

MARK TWAIN IN 1853 (*above*), *a
tintype made in the year he left
Hannibal to work in New York.*

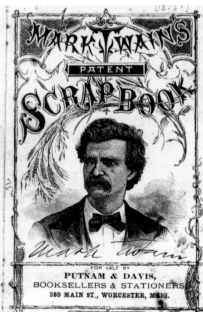

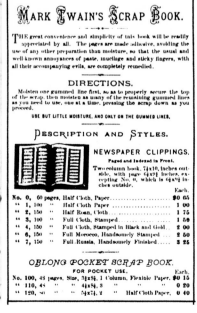

THE PATENT SCRAPBOOK (*left*),
*invented by Twain in 1861.
Throughout his life he was to
invest in money-making ventures,
many of which came to nothing.*

whether you do right or wrong, a person's conscience ain't got no sense, and just goes for him *anyway*. If I had a yaller dog that didn't know more than a person's conscience does, I would pison him. It takes up more room than all the rest of a person's insides, and yet ain't no good, nohow." (How the Lancashire annotator of my copy of *The Innocents Abroad* would have reacted to the morality of that passage can be imagined.) Like his guilt, not all of the unhappiness in his life was self-inflicted or, more accurately, was the result of his heredity and his complex personality. Much was the product of the domestic disasters to

which humanity is inevitably prone, but it was none the less traumatic for that.

Typically, before leaving Missouri in 1861, he had registered the patent for an invention of his own, a self-pasting scrapbook. His restless and boundless energy was to involve him in many schemes for augmenting the income from his books by ventures such as this, but, like Orion, he had something of his father's commercial flair for backing the wrong enterprises. As publisher, as investor, as patron of others, he made a great deal of money in his lifetime but he lost even more. Even these experiences, however, provided him with material on which to capitalize in his fiction, if only by involving him with a range of plausible, lovable optimists, often with more than a hint of roguery about them.

Throughout an often frenetic variety of simultaneous careers, Clemens remained the rough diamond that his humble origins and early attempts at finding a trade made him, but marriage, fame and rapidly increasing wealth strengthened at an early stage his aspirations towards social respectability. His impish sense of humour and his unfamiliarity with some of the prevailing social codes (as well as his impatience with them) made him perpetually liable to gaffes in his behaviour and in his writings. This

EXTERIOR AND INTERIOR OF "STORMFIELD", *Mark Twain's hilltop house at Redding, Connecticut (left). The earnings from his serialized autobiography enabled Twain to build this Italianate villa, his last home. John Howells, the architect who designed it, was the son of Twain's old friend, William Dean Howells.*

created a sense of insecurity embarrassing to the man but often useful to the writer: it increased his affinities with many of the unforgettable fictional characters he created with such humorous understanding.

As he grew older a sombre side to his nature darkened into a pessimism not unlike that of Jonathan Swift. The blackness of some of his late works, induced by personal disasters such as bereavements and bankruptcy, as well as by a world-weary disillusion with mankind's apparently universal inability to create a decent society, surprises many readers by the savageness of its bitter satire. This can also show itself in his better-known books, though again not always to the advantage of their consistency and artistic unity. *A Connecticut Yankee at King Arthur's Court* in particular suffers from this.

Yet his books have attracted, in our own time, an increasing amount of international scholarly analysis and documentation sometimes regarded by the unsympathetic as excessive. Mark Twain's papers are scattered, in varying quantities, through dozens of libraries all over the world. The largest single collection, at the University of Cali-

OLIVIA LANGDON CLEMENS *(above). An invalid for much of the thirty-four years of her marriage whose death in 1904 Twain described as "the disaster of my life".*

TWAIN AND OLIVIA
TRAVELLING, 1895 *(left). In
July 1895 Twain embarked on a
successful worldwide lecture tour,
taking in North America,
Australia, India and South
Africa. It was on his return to
England in July 1896 that he
learned that his beloved daughter
Susy had died of meningitis in
Hartford.*

MARK TWAIN MONUMENT
*(below), erected by the State of
Missouri at Florida, the writer's
birthplace. The bust was sculpted
by R. P. Bringhurst.*

fornia at Berkeley, is essential to any serious scholar. For the less specialist reader the collection of papers and memorabilia at the Mark Twain Memorial at Hartford, Connecticut, has the advantage of being housed in the bizarre mansion his first fortune enabled him to build in 1874, now faithfully maintained as a very congenial museum. Similarly, the little town of Hannibal, Missouri, has predictably been developed into a popular and informative tourist centre, while, for those prepared to undertake the thirty-mile drive into the hinterland, the Mark Twain Birthplace Shrine at Florida also has many attractions, including, lovingly preserved under cover, the cabin in which Samuel Langhorne Clemens was born. Yet to readers as well as to tourists, Mark Twain still has a great deal of enjoyment and interest to offer.

THE CELEBRATED JUMPING
FROG AND OTHER SKETCHES
THE INNOCENTS ABROAD
ROUGHING IT

Nummer 36.   Erscheint jeden Sonntag.   Wien, IX., Frankgasse 10.   Erscheint jeden Sonntag.   5. December 1897.

Ein Siegeszug des Humors.

(Text innstehend.)

Mark Twain hält eine humoristische Vorlesung im Goldgräberlager.

MARK TWAIN AND THE AMERICAN WEST

That so many of Mark Twain's best books are set in a nostalgically re-membered past is not merely sen-timentality on his part. The Civil War was to prove as significant a watershed in Mark Twain's own history as in his country's. When tensions between the North and the South had reached their final uneasy re-solution in 1865 with the abolition of that slavery about which the young Clemens had not realized there was anything wrong, not only was the Old South dead but the North too was radically different. America, however, could at least turn westwards to the challenge of developing the remainder of the continent. Clemens was already there and involved in the process. War had also had its not unusual side-effect of accelerat-ing technological change, notably in trans-portation. On 10 May 1869, at Promontory Point, Utah, the Union Pacific Railroad's track from the east finally and cere-moniously connected with the Central Paci-fic's line from California, thus completing the transcontinental rail link that Walt Whitman was to hail as forming a "Passage to India". Improvements in marine en-gineering had shortened the time and heightened the comfort of crossing the Atlantic which the telegraph had bridged as early as 1858. The world was shrinking and the times were changing.

In 1861, when the Clemens brothers set out from St Joseph for Nevada, the Union Pacific's track had not reached there. They were therefore obliged to travel by the established method of stagecoach and to take almost three weeks to cover the dis-

tance. Mark Twain's generation was the last to have grown up in the neighbourly, small-town, ante-bellum America.

In the process of adjusting to the ever-increasing momentum of the mechanized, urbanized, commercialized post-war socie-ty, it is hardly surprising that many writers before Whitman were tempted to take what he called "A Backward Glance O'er

MARK TWAIN ENTERTAINING GOLDMINERS (*opposite*). *This illustration from a Viennese publication of December 1897 depicts Twain, on the mining frontier of California thirty years earlier, holding spellbound an audience of miners. It is a tribute to his reputation in Austria as a raconteur and a Westerner, even after the publication of his more famous books on the Old South.*

THE IMPORTANCE OF RAIL TRANSPORT (*left*) *had been highlighted by the cost of moving troops and horseback during the American Civil War. Four years after the war ended, the east and west coasts of North America were linked by rail.*

TELEGRAPH OPERATOR (*below*). *The first successful transatlantic cable was laid between Ireland and Newfoundland in 1858, providing instant communication between Europe and North America.*

THE CASEMENT BROTHERS, *Jack (top above) and Dan (above) were responsible for laying a large part of the Union Pacific Railroad's track. They gathered together gangs of labourers with merciless efficiency.*

THE OREGON TRAIL (*right*) *by Albert Bierstadt (1830–1902). A member of parties originally surveying the new territories, Bierstadt became an early authority on its scenery. His huge romantic landscapes made him world famous.*

Travel'd Roads". The mining frontier, the excitement of which had lured eager prospectors in the gold rushes of the 1840s, was becoming more civilized as well as more populous. Although not themselves "forty-niners", the Clemenses were there early enough to identify with the old West, but also to become involved in its disappearance. Civilization called for social organization of the territories, in the provision of which Orion played a modest part. Newspapers were an essential feature of civilization: Sam helped to fuel those and his own imagination simultaneously.

Inevitably he succumbed initially to the Nevada lure of making a quick fortune by the discovery of a rich vein of silver or even gold. Equally inevitably he failed in the attempt: in that respect the family ill-luck held. Indirectly, his experiences were to prove more lucrative in shaping his career as a writer. Realizing early that there was no real role for him in association with Orion, he walked a hundred and thirty miles to Virginia City in 1862 to become a cub reporter at twenty-five dollars a week for the *Territorial Enterprise*. The editor, Joe Goodman, had already published a few humorous pieces by him, over the pen-name "Josh".

Now, though, Goodman sent him back to Carson City to report on the activities of the legislature: "I wrote a weekly letter to the paper: it appeared Sundays, and on Mondays the legislative proceedings were obstructed by the complaints of members as a result." It was to those letters, he claims, that he first appended the pseudonym "Mark Twain" (possibly out of consideration for Orion's position). Like his slightly earlier British counterpart, Charles Dickens, he began his literary career as, in effect, a parliamentary reporter. He might well have borrowed Dickens's words to sum up what that experience taught him: "My faith in the people governing is, on the whole, infinitesimal; my faith in the people governed is on the whole illimitable." Certainly, both writers grounded much of their satiric comedy in a healthy irreverence towards the received views and practices of what is now called "the Establishment".

The *Enterprise* had a reputation for racy and provocative journalism to which the new recruit responded warmly. This soon won him the respect and friendship of his colleagues, one of whom, however, seemed to the editor more talented and promising as a writer than Clemens. The latter he thought undeniably gifted but eccentric and lacking energy. The name of the other was William Wright, but he wrote as "Dan de Quille", with the Western humorists' enthusiasm for outlandish pen-names. By comparison with "Petroleum V. Nasby", "Orpheus C. Kerr" (a pun on "office-seeker") or the better-known "Artemus Ward", "Mark Twain" seems an unassuming choice. Easy-going and "one of the lads" in his social life, Clemens offended the editor of the *Union* with some of his articles and in May 1864 characteristically challenged him to a duel. He then discovered that this had recently become a felony in Nevada and so, rapidly but prudently, removed himself from the reach of the state law to California.

Not every state seems to have been as strict in its legislation. Almost thirty years later a similar clash between two Ohio editors culminated in a street shoot-out in which only one of them was shot but three passers-by were hit. The dryness of the *Herald Tribune's* reporting of it is worthy of Mark Twain himself: "The laws of Ohio ought not to allow a man to take charge of a newspaper unless he can shoot straight enough to hit his opponent and avoid hitting innocent persons."

In San Francisco Clemens was taken on by the *Morning Call* but found himself more circumscribed and constrained than in Virginia City: "After . . . scraping material together, I took the pen and spread this muck out into words and phrases and made it cover as much acreage as I could. It was fearful drudgery, soulless drudgery, and almost destitute of interests." His more literal muck-raking into the seamier aspects of public and business life in California led to exposés which he was obliged to send back to the *Enterprise* for publication because the *Call* would not touch them. Six months after arriving in San Francisco he was once again in the thick of controversy that threatened to turn so ugly that it became advisable for him to return temporarily to mining. This time he withdrew to the Tuolumne area where a friend, Jim Gillis, was already mining and where coinci-

ECHO CANYON (far left) "was like a long, smooth, narrow street, with a gradual descending grade, and shut in by enormous perpendicular walls of coarse conglomerate, four hundred feet high in many places, and turreted like mediaeval castles" (Roughing It).

THE FIRST PONY EXPRESS LEAVING ST JOSEPH, MISSOURI, *3 April 1860 (above left). "There was no idling time for a pony-rider on duty. He rode fifty miles without stopping, by daylight, moonlight, starlight, or through the blackness of darkness"* (Roughing It).

OFFICE OF THE *TERRITORIAL ENTERPRISE, still preserved in Virginia City (above). After an unsuccessful year of silvermining, Twain began working for this paper as a cub reporter in 1862. It was here that he first used the pseudonym "Mark Twain".*

A LOG HUT *(left) of the kind built by settlers and prospectors in the West when Twain found himself gripped by silver-fever in 1861.*

dence, with an arm longer than the law's, again aided him by introducing him to a tall tale that he made his first masterpiece.

How far his dissatisfaction with the *Call* and its drudgery was accelerated by something else is speculative, but what is a fact is that already there was a flourishing literary culture in San Francisco producing two significant periodicals, *The Golden Era* and *The Californian*. Clemens was already involved in this activity, and stimulated by it. In February 1865 it seemed safe to return from Tuolumne to the Bay, but his only post now was as the *Enterprise's* correspondent, so the need for additional income may have heightened his natural ambition to write more for the literary journals. In response to a request from "Artemus

Ward" (Charles Farrar Browne) for a comic sketch for inclusion in an anthology, he wrote up the story he had collected in the hills, but, lethargic as ever, missed the publisher's deadline. This too may have been providential for, anxious not to waste it, Clemens offered the piece to the *New York Saturday Press*, where it was published on 18 November 1865. In a West Coast humorous anthology the piece might well have stood out less conspicuously than in the prominence of the East Coast paper where it provided an instant sensation. As was the custom, other newspapers nationwide promptly reprinted it.

The story was originally entitled "Jim Smiley and His Jumping Frog", although since 1867, when it appeared in, and gave its title to, a book of Mark Twain's tales, it became known as "The Celebrated Jumping Frog of Calaveras County". The skilful

ARTEMUS WARD *(above), the pen-name of Charles Farrar Browne (1834–67), a Western humorist who achieved great popularity in Britain as well as North America.*

THE CLIFFS, SAN FRANCISCO *(above). Having moved to California in 1864, Twain wrote humorous pieces for two San Francisco literary journals and continued to act as correspondent for the* Enterprise.

GOLDMINING IN CALIFORNIA *(right), c. 1870, lithograph by Currier and Ives. "We lived in a small cabin on a verdant hillside, and there were not five other cabins in view over the wide expanse of hill and forest"* (Roughing It).

use of narrators was to become a respected feature of Mark Twain's way of presenting a story. Here he begins in the first person, giving an effect of authenticity, by describing his meeting in a mining camp with "good-natured, garrulous old Simon Wheeler". Wheeler then takes over the narration of the main anecdote himself, but not before Mark Twain has attributed to him recognizable characteristics of what was to become his own style in print and on the lecture platform throughout his life:

He never smiled, he never frowned, he never changed his voice from the gentle-flowing key to which he tuned his initial sentence, he never betrayed the slightest suspicion of enthusiasm, but all through the interminable narrative there ran a vein of impresive earnestness and sincerity which showed me plainly that, so far from his imagining that there was anything ridiculous or funny about his story, he regarded it as a really important matter and admired its two heroes as men of transcendent genius in *finesse*.

Loquaciously, with digressions and subsidiary anecdotes, Wheeler establishes Jim Smiley as an inveterate gambler who would bet on anything "if he could get anybody to bet on the other side, and if he couldn't he'd change sides". Smiley had "a little small bull-pup", a champion fighter who would let his opponent make the running until all the bets were laid, and then "Andrew Jackson – which was the name of the pup" would seize the other dog by his hind leg and tenaciously retain the grip until the other gave in. Andrew Jackson remained undefeated until a challenger fielded against him a dog "that didn't have no hind legs, because they'd been sawed off in a circular saw". With nothing to seize hold of, the champion "got shucked out bad. He gave Smiley a look, as much as to say his heart was broke . . . and then he limped off a piece and laid down and died."

The technique is perfect: the poker-faced production of outrageous circumstantial detail, naming the dog after the American President known as "Old Hickory" because of his toughness, and crediting the animal with human attributes including dying of despair. And then, for full measure, this is repeated in the central story of the frog Smiley turned into a bet-winning jumper:

Smiley said all a frog wanted was education and he could do "most anything – and I believe him. Why, I've seen him set Dan'l Webster down here on this floor – Dan'l Webster was the name of the frog – and sing out "Flies, Dan'l, flies!" and quicker'n you could wink he'd spring straight up and snake a fly off'n the counter there, and flop down on the floor ag'in as solid as a gob of mud, and fall to scratching the side of his head with his hind foot as indifferent as if he hadn't no idea he'd been doin' any more'n any frog might do. You never see a frog so modest and straightfor'ard as he was, for all he was so gifted.

Here the technique is enriched by the vividly colloquial metaphor of the "gob of mud", the detail of the frog's movements, and again its moral attributes, but above all by

LOST IN THE SNOW (*opposite, top*). "I rose up, and there in the gray dawn, not fifteen steps from us, were the frame buildings of a stage station" (Roughing It).

DAY DREAMS (*left*): "my mind had work on hand, and it labored on diligently, night and day, whether my hands were idle or employed" (Roughing It).

CENTRAL PACIFIC WHARF, SAN FRANCISCO (*left*). In 1866 Twain was sent from California to the Sandwich Islands (now Hawaii) by the Sacramento Union to report on the area.

31

CHLORIDE CAVE, LION HILL *(above), in the mining district near Salt Lake City, Utah.*

THE GREAT SALT LAKE, UTAH *(right). "We desired to visit the famous inland sea, the American 'Dead Sea,' the great Salt Lake – seventeen miles, horseback, from the city – for we had dreamed about it, and thought about it, and talked about it"* (Roughing It).

the genuineness of the oral delivery in Wheeler's own vernacular.

Then comes a challenger who has at first no frog to field. Rather than lose the chance of a bet, Smiley departs to find him one, leaving the wily stranger free to work on Dan'l Webster: he "prized his mouth open and took a teaspoon and filled him full of quail-shot – filled him pretty near up to his chin – and set him on the floor". Smiley returns with a frog and the two are aligned:

Him and the feller touched up the frogs from behind, and the new frog hopped off lively, but Dan'l give a heave and hysted up his shoulders – so – like a Frenchman, but it warn't no use – he couldn't budge; he was planted as solid as a church, and he couldn't no more stir than if he was anchored out.

The defeat by trickery of the modest, straightfor'ard and gifted frog tacitly gives the story the aura of a parable, but our immediate response is to the humour. This time a visual element is introduced with the imitation of the frog's action, made more vivid by the unexpectedly cosmopolitan simile of the Frenchman, but as always the effect relies on the convincing cadences and vocabulary of the speaking voice. Only when the indefatigable Wheeler launches on yet another anecdote ("Well, thish-yer Smiley had a yaller one-eyed cow that didn't have no tail, only just a short stump like a

bannanner, and – ") do the original narrator and the reader, "lacking both time and inclination", take their leave.

"The Jumping Frog" brought Mark Twain's name into the public eye, but before tracing his career further it is appropriate, if not chronologically strictly accurate, to turn to his second book, *Roughing It*, published in 1872. This conveniently recapitulates his journey to and life on the Nevada frontier and in San Francisco. Between "The Jumping Frog" and *Roughing It* there had been the instantly successful *The Innocents Abroad*, but the relationship between the two books is close enough for Mark Twain to have used *The Innocents at Home* as the title for the second volume of the two-part English edition of *Roughing It* which slightly preceded the publication of the one-volume first American edition. Both exploit comically the discrepancy between expectation and experience – the supreme, brash self-confidence of human beings, despite their utter inability to foresee or cope with the new, the unexpected or even the unfamiliar.

In both cases the book is structurally determined primarily by the journey which each describes. This is enlivened by graphic and lighthearted accounts of the places seen, the experiences undergone and the people met. If "The Jumping Frog" established Mark Twain's potential as a short story writer, it is not merely hindsight to see in these two books the potential novelist.

Historically it was from such beginnings that the European picaresque novel developed – the anecdotal account of the journey that brings the narrator into contact with sections of society utterly unfamiliar to him (usually the poor and often the rogues). Unity is given to the string of incidents by a plot interest that need be no more than minimal, but mainly by the persona of the narrator, the innocent for whom the whole experience is disturbing but highly educative. The narrator of *The Innocents Abroad* and *Roughing It* is something of a latter-day Don Quixote, and, much as the Victorian in Clemens disliked what he saw as the grossness of eighteenth-century English fiction, Huckleberry Finn actually has a lot in common with Henry Fielding's Joseph Andrews.

The 'I' of *Roughing It* follows the route of Sam Clemens from St Joseph, Missouri, to Salt Lake City, and on across the desert to the mining territory of Nevada where he experiences the heady excitements and disappointments of the "flush times", and turns to journalism in Virginia City. The narrator journeys on to California where, in San Francisco, his fortunes continue to fluctuate until a journalistic assignment takes him unexpectedly to the Sandwich Islands. Factually, of course, it is Clemens's

career, but the persona of the innocent is sustained throughout.

The most celebrated anecdote of innocence in *Roughing It* is the one in Chapter XXIV in which Mark Twain is gulled by an auctioneer's brother into buying as a bargain a horse, about which he is later told: "'He is the very worst devil to buck on the continent of America . . . And moreover, he is a simon-pure, out-and-out, genuine d----d Mexican plug, and an uncommon mean one at that too.'" Having already learnt that lesson the hard way he restrains his comments to: "I gave no sign; but I made up my mind that if the auctioneer's brother's funeral took place while I was in the Territory I would postpone all other recreations and attend it."

Mark Twain is to survive and laugh at many such incidents before the book finishes. The new frontier has awakened constant new enthusiasms and expectations which, the reader suspects as the book ends, have only to be fulfilled for Samuel Clemens before the "I" resumes in another book a story that he is now reluctantly suspending only for want of further copy.

Nevertheless, convention requires a conclusion: "Thus, after seven years of vicissitudes, ended a 'pleasure trip' to the silver mines of Nevada which had originally been

FIRE AT LAKE TAHOE *(above).* "*We were driven to the boat by the intense heat, and there we remained spell-bound. Within half an hour all before us was a tossing, blinding tempest of flame!*" (Roughing It).

DANCE OF THE MEN OF THE SANDWICH ISLES *(left). During his half-year trip to the islands, Twain visited Honolulu, Hawaii, and Maui, and lectured on his travels after his return to the United States.*

NINETEENTH-CENTURY MAP OF EUROPE *(opposite) by John Tallis. In 1866 the editor of the* Alta California *commissioned Twain to write a weekly humorous travel letter from Europe and the Middle East.*

intended to occupy only three months." What differentiates the "I" from Clemens is the addition of the wry sentence "However, I usually miss my calculations by more than that", and the compunction to satisfy moralistic expectations:

MORAL

If the reader thinks he is done, now, and that this book has no moral to it, he is in error. The moral of it is this: If you are of any account, stay at home and make your way by faithful diligence; but if you are "no account", go away from home, and then you will *have* to work, whether you want to or not. Thus you become a blessing to your friends by ceasing to be a nuisance to them – if the people you go among suffer by the operation.

SHOSHONEES WITH ANNUITY GOODS *(right). Before travelling westwards Twain had conceived an unreal picture of the native Americans, viewed "through the mellow moonshine of romance" offered by writers like Fenimore Cooper.*

NATIVE AMERICANS *(below) were employed in building the railroads, "a class who have a hard enough time of it in the pitiless deserts of the Rocky Mountains"* (Roughing It).

Acclimatized by now to Mark Twain's style, the reader of *Roughing It* is aware of the characteristically dry exaggeration of the narrator's self-deprecatory admission of inadequacy, the irony which quietly subverts a moral superficially Franklinian, and the fact that, for Clemens, the seven years cannot in reality have been the hilarious picnic that the book has suggested.

Yet, even less than *The Innocents Abroad* can *Roughing It* be categorized as a purely comic work. Both books seek to inform as well as to entertain the reader, but with one difference. *The Innocents Abroad* deals with Europe and the Holy Land, to both of which there was an accepted respectful response already familiar to the American audience and therefore an easy target for Mark Twain's ridicule. To the virgin land to which he turned his attention in his second book there was as yet no accepted response other than vague wonder and uninformed curiosity. To ridicule that curiosity would be neither generous nor desirable, but, as a professional humorist, he cannot resist heightening the reader's wonder with a number of traveller's stories that border on the tall tale, but are told with the poker-faced gravity he exploited when lecturing.

Thus, Chapter XXXVIII contains an account of the "Thoughtless Act of our Dog, and the Results" in the strongly alkaline water of Lake Mono. Already having "more raw places on him than sound ones", the dog misguidedly jumped in, and then promptly tried to correct his error:

He yelped and barked and howled as he went – and by the time he got to the shore there was no bark to him – for he had barked the bark all out of his inside, and the alkali water had cleaned the bark all off his outside, and he probably wished he had never embarked in any such enterprise. He ran round and round in a circle, and pawed the earth and clawed the air, and threw double somersaults, sometimes backward and sometimes forward, in the most extraordinary manner. He was not a demonstrative dog, as a general thing, but rather of a grave and serious turn of mind, and I never saw him take so much interest in anything before. He finally struck out over the mountains, at a gait which we estimated at about two hundred and fifty miles an hour, and he is going yet. This was about nine years ago. We look for what is left of him along here every day.

At the same time, by preserving the persona of the innocent that had served him so well

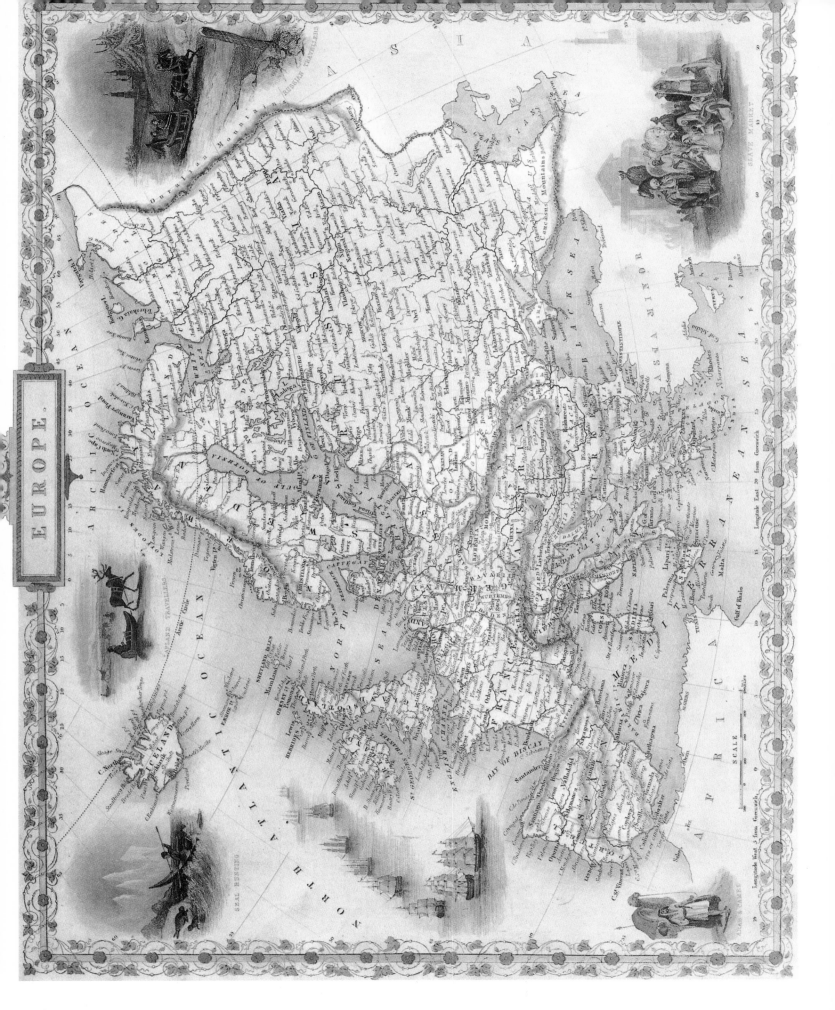

EUROPE.

ASIA

RUSSIAN TRAVELLERS

SLAVE MARKET

ASIA MINOR

ARCTIC OCEAN

WHITE SEA

GULF OF FINLAND

MOSCOW

BLACK SEA

CAUCASUS

CASPIAN SEA

LAPLAND TRAVELLERS

ICELAND

SHETLAND ISLES

NORTH SEA

ENGLISH CHANNEL

BAY OF BISCAY

FRANCE

SPAIN

MEDITERRANEAN SEA

AFRICA

NORTH ATLANTIC OCEAN

SEAL HUNTING

SCALE

Longitude West 5 from Greenwich.   Longitude East 20 from Greenwich. 25

in the previous book, he can (as in "The Jumping Frog") pass other anecdotes off as having been told to him by men of experience. This at once gives them some validity, however dubious, and the reader then has the added amusement of recognizing that the narrator is himself also gullible enough to have been the victim of jokers, as in the case of the "marvellous Whiteman cement mine" reputed to lie near Lake Mono.

The desire to impart serious information Mark Twain makes light of in his Preface: "Yes, take it all around, there is quite a good deal of information in the book. I regret this very much; but really it could not be helped: information appears to stew out of me naturally, like the precious ottar of roses out of the otter." Trying to reconcile this light-heartedness at times with a more serious approach presents Mark Twain with more difficulty, as in the matter of the Goshute Indians (he spells it "Goshoot"). His hostile and patronizing attitude to them is of its time, though it is neatly turned into an attack on the false expectations about the "Noble Red Man" implanted by Fenimore Cooper, to the unreality of whose romances Mark Twain was implacably opposed,

though Samuel Clemens obviously knew those romances well. Nevertheless, such sympathy as he finds for the Indians is uncomfortably ambivalent in its expression: "They deserve pity, poor creatures; and they can have mine – at this distance. Nearer by, they never get anybody's", for, at closer quarters, they are "treacherous, filthy and repulsive". No less disparagingly racist towards the Indians of Utah, was the 1877 diary of a British Wesleyan minister, returning to his missionary work in China by sea to New York and train to San Francisco.

Mark Twain, however, trying to leaven his censure with humour, refers to "an impression abroad that the Baltimore and Washington Railway Company and many of its employés are Goshoots; but it is an error". So, one feels, is his allusion to it. He is hinting at the custom of using pejoratively the name of a despised people to vilify others, condemning it in this case only by suggesting that the railway men are worse than Goshoots. It detracts most unfortunately from what might have been the intended sincerity of his concluding sentiment: "If we cannot find it in our hearts to give those poor naked creatures our Christ-

VERNAL FALLS, NEAR VIRGINIA CITY (*above*). *Centre of an important mining area, Virginia City overlooked "a vast far-reaching panorama of mountain ranges and deserts"* (Roughing It).

LIFE ON THE PRAIRIE — THE BUFFALO HUNT (*right*), *a lithograph of 1862, artist unknown. "It was noble sport galloping over the plain in the dewy freshness of the morning"* (Roughing It).

ian sympathy and compasssion, in God's name let us at least not throw mud at them." The attitudes of the 1990s must not be expected of the 1870s, and *Roughing It* is an early work of its author's, but he was always prone to these occasional lapses of judgement and taste.

A method he uses to document and authenticate information seriously imparted is to insert extracts from printed sources either in the text or as appendices. Western newspapers are drawn on, and so, in the section on Salt Lake City which aims at some degree of objectivity, is the Mormon Bible – several times and at length. Nevertheless, warning the reader immediately before the first of those Mormon extracts that "It is chloroform in print" is hardly calculated to engage his close attention.

These are minor blemishes in proportion to the book's impact as a whole. What is invaluable in it is its first-hand, articulate, balanced retrospect on perhaps the most idealized episode in American history, the opening up of the Golden West. It is not coincidental that the finest of recent Mark Twain scholars, Henry Nash Smith, should also have written that seminal work, *Virgin Land: the American West as Symbol and Myth*. It is to Mark Twain's credit that, in *Roughing It* especially, he recognizes, as early as 1872, that the frontier was already a myth twenty years before Frederick Jackson Turner was to formulate his frontier thesis. Nor must Mark Twain's nostalgic contribution to that myth overlay his awareness of the sordid, mean violence, greed and inhumanity that accompanied the more heroic endeavours.

RINGING FOR SOAP (*left*). *The American tourists soon got used to many aspects of European travel, but not to having to ring for soap.* "We think of it just after we get our heads and faces thoroughly wet, or just when we have been in the bath-tub long enough" (The Innocents Abroad).

Chapter LVII is a threnody for the passing of the Old West as eloquent as anything Mark Twain ever wrote, especially the lengthy passage that begins:

It was a driving, vigorous, restless population in those days. It was a *curious* population. It was the *only* population of the kind that the world has ever seen gathered together, and it is not likely that the world will ever see its like again.

Yet even this celebration of a young, energetic, all-male society ends with the recognition that "they were rough in those times . . . It was a wild, free, disorderly, grotesque society!" and Chapters XLVIII to L have already documented that vividly.

The popularity of the book in the West is amusingly attested to by the British Wesleyan missionary already mentioned: in Milton, California, he was told of a service held locally where the congregation had broken down in the middle of the Lord's Prayer, having forgotten the words, but had been rescued by someone finding the text of it in a copy of *Roughing It*. The missionary himself seems to have been something of a connoisseur of American Western humour, for, of a Methodist temperance service in San Francisco, he comments: "One of the speakers was a simple Artemus Ward for dry drollery." Such references substantiate Bret Harte's indications, in stories such as

CROSSING THE ATLANTIC (*left*) "*I said: 'Good-morning, sir. It is a fine day.' He put his hand on his stomach and said 'Oh, my!' and then staggered away and fell over the coop of a sky-light*" (The Innocents Abroad).

MOROCCAN TRADERS (*above*) *by Publio de Tommali (b. 1849). In the streets of Tangier Twain found an* Arabian Nights *world, with "all sorts of people that are foreign and curious . . ."*

The relevance of the chapters on the Sandwich Islands (as Hawaii was then known) to a book primarily about the Frontier could be more rigorously questioned were it not that they mark the culmination of Clemens's own western experience. His visit was a journalistic assignment by the Sacramento *Union* in 1866 for him to write a set of letters home about this exotic and almost legendary area. Since, at that time, the American West itself was hardly less exotic and legendary, the re-use of the letters to form these chapters is not wholly inappropriate. Out of any new experience Mark Twain's fertile imagination was always ready to create literature, and the letters had already consolidated his reputation as a humorist.

Moreover, the persona of the unsophisticated traveller, thirsting for, yet almost always disappointed by, exposure to unfamiliar places also unifies the two sections of *Roughing It.* And unsophisticated his response to the Sandwich Islands, and especially to their inhabitants, certainly is. That foreign parts and foreign people are by definition funny is a belief not yet totally erased from the minds of the untravelled. In the nineteenth century it was so widespread as to present the humorist with an opportunity he could not resist, though at times one wishes he had. Uneasy at the uninhibited nudity of the natives, he underplays their patent innocence in order to mock the uses to which they put some of the garments given to them by embarrassed missionaries, and then pokes fun at the missionaries for expecting anything different. Elsewhere he amuses his reader with innuendo: "I came upon a bevy of nude native young ladies bathing in the sea, and went and sat down upon their clothes to keep them from being stolen. I begged them to come out, for the sea was rising . . . But they were not afraid, and presently went on with their sport."

Harmless fun, but unsubtle and overindulged, although in the original *Union* letter on which this is based it was even cruder. Similarly puns like the "ottar"/ "otter" of the Preface recur constantly. For example, the phrase "squatting on their hams" is introduced in order to produce this rather laboured parenthesis: "(The Sandwich Islanders always squat on their

"The Outcasts of Poker Flat" and poems like "Dickens in Camp", of a frontier interest in reading, rather in the way that a derelict mine in Colorado is still "The Dolly Varden", named after the Dickens heroine about whom Harte also wrote a poem.

hams, and who knows but they may be the old original 'ham sandwiches'? The thought is pregnant with interest.)" The greater virtuosity with which he sustains the "bark" pun in the story of the dog in Lake Mono earlier in the book illustrates his literary development between the letters for the *Union* in 1866, from which he reprints the "ham sandwich" parenthesis verbatim, and the writing of *Roughing It* a few years later. Describing himself and his friends, at the end of their Western experience, as "centless as the last rose of summer", he excuses it neatly: "That is a poor joke, but it is in pathetic harmony with the circumstances, since we were so poor ourselves."

It was this sort of humour that his audiences wanted, however, and the popularity of these letters encouraged the editor of the *Alta California* at the end of the year to commission him to extend his geographical range by joining a pleasure trip to Europe and to produce a similar series from that. It was the success of those in their turn that Mark Twain, always ready to maximize the profits of experience, was three years later to turn into his first book, *The Innocents Abroad*. To discuss this book in a chapter dealing with Twain's life in the West is less quixotic than it seems; for his whole attitude to Europe is dictated by his frontier outlook, as the frequency of his references to the West throughout makes clear.

The ending of the American Civil War

A DECIDED SHAVE (*above*). "*From earliest infancy it had been a cherished ambition of mine to be shaved some day in a palatial barber-shop of Paris . . . The truth is, as I believe I have since found out, that they have no barber-shops worthy of the name*" (The Innocents Abroad).

MARSEILLE, THE CATHEDRAL, C. 1880 (*left*). "*Toward nightfall, the next evening, wes steamed into the great artificial harbour of this noble city of Marseilles, and saw the dying sunlight gild its clustering spires and ramparts*" (The Innocents Abroad).

PONT DU CARROUSEL, WITH
THE LOUVRE, PARIS (above).
*Having hired a guide to take him
to the Louvre, Twain found
himself being inveigled into a
tour of the shops, not guessing
that the man was being paid a
percentage on all sales by the
shopkeepers* (The Innocents
Abroad).

AMERICAN DRUNKS, PARIS
*(right). Having found a bar that
advertised "All Manner of
American Drinks Artistically
Prepared Here", Twain was
disappointed to discover that the
waiter could not speak English*
(The Innocents Abroad).

and the improvement in sea travel had
revived the pre-war enthusiasm of wealthy
Americans for the tour of Europe that was
to provide novelists like Henry James with
such rich material. The promotion of the
six-month, two-thousand dollar excursion
of the *Quaker City* was, in actuality, every bit
as high-powered as the opening chapters of
The Innocents Abroad suggest, breezy as the
presentation of them is. General William T.
Sherman, famous for having led the Union
forces across Georgia to Atlanta and on to
the sea in 1864–5, did indeed lend his name
to it. The eminent minister, Henry Ward
Beecher, at the height of his reputation and
still seven years away from the allegations of
adultery that later made him the subject of
scandal, only withdrew when he found his
name was being used as publicity.

The sequence of subsequent chapters in
the book follows the stages of the tour. The
initial preparations and the voyage out lead
to the Straits of Gibraltar; brief visits to
Morocco and Marseilles are followed by a
longer visit to Paris. In Chapter XVII we
arrive in Italy where we remain for a furth-

THE BAY OF NAPLES *(left)*. *Although Twain thought Naples from a distance extremely impressive, he found the "contrasts between opulence and poverty, and magnificence and misery" on its streets less romantic* (The Innocents Abroad).

THE FRENCH CAN-CAN, c. 1899, *lithograph by Pierre Vidal. Twain's description of his reactions to the version he saw some thirty years earlier alternates between outrage and fascination.*

MARK TWAIN *(bottom right) by Carroll Beckwith (1890). Twain must have looked much like this, corncob pipe and all, in his days in Nevada and California.*

PLYMOUTH CHURCH, BROOKLYN *(bottom), parish of the Rev. Henry Ward Beecher.*

THE REV. HENRY WARD BEECHER *(below) who was to have accompanied the voyagers on the* Quaker City.

er fifteen chapters, and are then whisked through Greece, on to Russia and back via Smyrna to Ephesus, all in a mere eight chapters, before we arrive at last at the high point of the tour, the Holy Land, where we spend sixteen chapters. Two chapters in Egypt, a particularly breathless one glimpsing Spain, Madeira and Bermuda, as well as the voyage home, and then, docking in New York, "the long, strange tour was over. Amen." The still-prevalent stereotype of the eager but uncomprehending American tourist "doing" Europe in the minimum time probably owes much to this work by America's most popular writer.

The American single-volume edition of 1869 was followed in 1870 by a London edition in two volumes. There was an interval of some six weeks between the appearance of the two parts, separately titled *The Innocents Abroad: The Voyage Out* and *The New Pilgrim's Progress: The Journey Home.* The division, dictated by the size of the whole, occurs irritatingly just over half-way through Italy.

The humour of the book relies on the separation of the tourists into two quite distinct categories. First there are the "Pilgrims", credulous and guide-book-clutching, indoctrinated with the received attitude of reverence towards the wonders of the past – especially the past of Europe and the Holy Land, and desperate to respond appropriately. Although many parishioners of Henry Ward Beecher had

withdrawn from the original list with their pastor, the fact that his was the Plymouth Church, Brooklyn, may have suggested the name "Pilgrims" to Clemens. Second, there are the "Boys", who are reluctant to be impressed by anything and remain immovably convinced of the unquestionable superiority of things American.

The two groups are both "Innocents" in different ways. The Pilgrims are guilelessly innocent in their unquestioning conformity. The Boys are innocent in their uninhibited freedom from any artificial and sophisticated notions. Mark Twain's home state of Missouri is sometimes referred to as the "Show me" state, from the folklore of the reluctance of people from Missouri to believe anything until it has been fully and explicitly shown to them. Although they are in that sense "from Missouri", the Boys will not necessarily accept something even when they have been shown it.

Mark Twain's sympathies are, predictably, with the Boys, but they fall short of complete identification. Like the Pilgrims, but more judiciously, he is susceptible to the combination of scenery and association that Europe presents to him:

"See Naples and die." Well, I do not know that one would necessarily die after merely seeing it, but to attempt to live there might turn out a little different-ly. To see Naples as we saw it in the early dawn from far up on the side of Vesuvius, is to see a picture of wonderful beauty. At that distance its dingy buildings looked white – and so, rank on rank of balconies, windows, and roofs, they piled themselves up from the blue ocean till the colossal castle of St Elmo topped the grand white pyramid and gave the picture symmetry, emphasis, and completeness. And when its lilies turned to roses – when it blushed under the sun's first kiss – it was beautiful beyond all descrip-tion. One might well say, then, "See Naples and die".

Mark Twain continues further in this vein and then immediately undercuts it with a vivid close-up of overcrowded, narrow, filthy streets full of "disagreeable sights and smells" breeding cholera. The overall im-pact of the book on the reader contemplat-ing travel is to encourage him, but with realistic warnings.

Understandably, he envisages an Amer-ican audience primarily, missing no chance of comparing nineteenth-century America favourably with picturesque Europe and even the Holy Land. His preference for Lake Tahoe (in his beloved territories of Nevada and California) for size and scenery to Lake Como and the Sea of Galilee is something his contemporary European readers probably took with less equanimity than we might, but even for them he had surprises in store.

In Paris Mark Twain professes outrage at "the renowned can-can", like which nothing "has been seen on earth since the trembling Tam O'Shanter saw the devil and the witch-es at their orgies". He tempers this, though,

by the admission: "I placed my hands be-fore my eyes for very shame. But I looked through my fingers." (Fielding used that joke in *Joseph Andrews*, and Mark Twain would not have been above borrowing it from him.) He gets, as one would expect, maximum comedy from the French inabil-ity to comprehend American English, all of which, like his irreverent version of the Heloise and Abelard story, is calculated to endear him to the Boys, as is his hostility to the Old Masters in art galleries whose repu-tation he constantly debunks, and so much more.

Yet, by the time the party has reached Milan in Chapter XIX, even the burlesque

ARCH OF CONSTANTINE, ROME *(top left). Having ascended to the summit of the dome of St Peter's, Twain was able to see every notable object in Rome, including "the ruins of temples, columns, and triumphal arches that knew the Caesars" (*The Innocents Abroad*).

THE SPANISH STEPS, ROME *(above). Twain found Rome a fascinating city, but felt himself while there to be "like a boy in a candy-shop – there was everything to choose from, and yet no choice" (*The Innocents Abroad*).

THE SHRINE OF THE HOLY
SEPULCHRE *(right), lithograph
by David Roberts RA, 1838. "the
most sacred locality on earth to
millions and millions of men, and
women, and children, the noble,
and the humble, bond and free.
In its history from the first, and
its tremendous associations, it is
the most illustrious edifice in
Christendom"* (The Innocents
Abroad).

of European guides with their inadequate Franglais ("Do you wis zo haut can be?" as an invitation to go to the top of a monument) is suspended for this unexpected and quite unequivocal tribute to Europeans and their way of life:

They go to bed moderately early, and sleep well. They are always quiet, always orderly, always cheerful, comfortable, and appreciative of life and its manifold blessings. One never sees a drunken man among them. The change that has come over our little party is surprising. Day by day we lose some of our restlessness and absorb some of the spirit of quietude and ease that is in the tranquil atmosphere about us and in the demeanor of the people. We grow wise apace. We begin to comprehend what life is for.

He is even "wishing we could export some of it to our restless, driving, vitality-consuming marts at home".

In Rome, seven short chapters later, he digresses from his narrative, not by any means for the first time. The frontier anecdote which he introduces is lengthy, and its relevance not immediately apparent, unless one recognizes a return to the theme of America's need to lose some of its restlessness and cultivate a wise tranquility of spirit.

Even more surprisingly, when the tourists meet the Russian royal family, Mark Twain's robust republicanism gives way to a similar respect for these qualities in them.

In Rome, his anecdote describes the tribulations of Judge Oliver, making a nightmare winter journey to take up an appointment as Probate Judge in Humboldt County, Nevada. The story is punctuated, at every vicissitude, with the words "But Oliver did not complain". Snowed up in a canyon, the party resorts to building a "Humboldt house" by creating a dugout in the side of a hill, and extending the ground space by stretching a canvas roof forward to two uprights. Sitting under this one night, relaxing by writing poetry beside the sagebrush fire, the Judge hears an animal moving about on the hillside near the roof, and shouts from time to time to frighten it off: "But by and by he fell asleep where he sat, and pretty soon a mule fell down the chimney! The fire flew in every direction, and Oliver went over backwards." Ten nights later it happens again, and again he does not complain. Instead he moves to a similar dwelling across the canyon where the mules do not seem to go:

JERUSALEM FROM THE MOUNT OF OLIVES *(below), lithograph by David Robers RA, c. 1839. "Perched on its eternal hills, white and domed and solid, massed together and hooped with high grey walls, the venerable city gleamed in the sun" (The Innocents Abroad).*

WAITER, SHEPHERD'S HOTEL
(above). Twain and his party
stayed in this Cairo hotel, which
he pronounced "the worst on
earth", although he did not
specify why (The Innocents
Abroad).

comment means either that he is being ridiculed as a man devoid of all proper emotional response or extolled as a man of remarkable self-control. Obviously, he is being presented as, *par excellence*, "a man that fortune's buffets and rewards / Has ta'en with equal thanks", and Mark Twain's respect for him, like Hamlet's for Horatio, is the respect of the man whose own soul is divided for the man of completely unified personality. In this respect, it is particularly difficult to separate Mark Twain from Samuel Clemens.

The same is true of the following chapter, in which he visits the Capuchin monastery and is fascinated by the charnel house, with its six divisions, each "ornamented with a style of decoration peculiar to itself – and these decorations were in every instance formed of human bones!" The bones, he learns, are those of all the former monks, many of whom the guide identifies and whose lives he describes graphically, before exhibiting the shrivelled bodies of other monks, still in their robes. The narrator's interest in the macabre modulates quickly into, again, a respect for single-minded equanimity:

I asked the monk if all the brethren up stairs expected to be put in this place when they died. He answered quietly:
"We must all lie here at last."
See what one can accustom himself to. The reflection that he must some day be taken apart like an engine or a clock, or like a house whose owner is gone, and worked up into arches and pyramids and hideous frescoes, did not distress this monk in the least. I thought he even looked as if he were thinking, with complacent vanity, that his own skull would look well on top of the heap and his own ribs add a charm to the frescoes which possibly they lacked at present.

One night about eight o'clock he was endeavouring to finish his poem, when a stone rolled in – then a hoof appeared below the canvas – then part of a cow – the after part. He leaned back in dread, and shouted "Hooy! hooy! get out of this!" and the cow struggled manfully – lost ground steadily – dirt and dust streamed down, and before Oliver could get well away, the entire cow crashed through on to the table and made a shapeless wreck of everything!

Then, for the first time in his life, I think, Oliver complained. He said:
"This thing is growing monotonous!"
Then he resigned his judgeship and left Humboldt county.

The inadequacy of the Judge's temperate

The Victorians, American or British, were, by our standards, lugubriously obsessed with death, but one hardly expects it to surface so extensively in a book by a celebrated humorist, despite the lightness which Mark Twain injects into the close of that passage. In the section on Paris the reader has already been conducted with morbid thoroughness around the morgue (immediately prior to the description of the can-can) and learned, in similar detail, that "One of our pleasantest visits was to Père la Chaise, the national burying ground of France", immediately before being con-

THE KING'S CHAMBER (*left*). "*A great stone sarcophagus like a bath-tub stood in the centre of the King's Chamber. Around it were gathered a picturesque group of Arab savages and soiled and tattered pilgrims, who held their candles aloft in the gloom*" (The Innocents Abroad).

soled with the burlesquing of Heloise and Abelard. The Boys, from the start, have derived much merriment, when confronted in museums by mummies and similar exhibits, from asking the guide in mock-seriousness "Is he dead?" Even on leaving the monastery Mark Twain can joke that "They were trying to keep from asking, 'Is – is he dead?'" It says much for his skill, and for his hypnotic hold on the reader, that he can handle such transitions so successfully.

It also indicates the appropriateness with which one can apply to Sam Clemens a phrase from Scott Fitzgerald's *The Great Gatsby*: "Almost any exhibition of complete self-sufficiency always draws a stunned tribute from me." The other side of his mercurial personality might, without extravagance, be seen as symbolized in the great interest he takes, in both his earliest travel books, in volcanoes: Vesuvius, Stromboli, and Kilauea in Hawaii, by comparison with which Vesuvius is "a soup-kettle". Not for nothing did Bernard DeVoto entitle a collection of the author's later and more vitriolically polemical pieces *Mark Twain in Eruption*. The cooled lava of Vesuvius "left to glower at heaven in impotent rage forevermore" and Kilauea in eruption giving off vapour that suggests "a released soul soaring homeward from captivity with the damned," are phrases resonant of the rage and world-weariness that were to torment

Clemens's later years. Indeed, it had already begun, for much later he was to recall a period during the writing of *Roughing It* as "among the blackest, the gloomiest, the most wretched of my long life".

From these early travels, however, three benefits, two of them quite unforeseeable, accrued to Clemens as a writer. The least unexpected was the opportunity that they gave him for a new career on the lecturing platform. In the penultimate chapter of *Roughing It* he describes the attempts of friends to dissuade him from something for which they thought him quite unfitted; he

THE COLOSSI OF THEBES (*left*). On leaving Egypt, Twain professed himself glad to have seen the land "*that walked in the broad highway of civilisation in the grey dawn of creation, ages and ages before we were born*" (The Innocents Abroad).

THE ASCENT OF VESUVIUS (right). We "started sleepily up the mountain, with a vagrant at each mule's tail who pretended to be driving the brute along, but was really holding on and getting himself dragged up instead" (The Innocents Abroad).

On board the *Quaker City* he made the acquaintance of a Mrs Mary Mason Fairbanks, only seven years his senior but the mother of two children and the wife of the proprietor of the *Cleveland Herald*, for which paper she was covering the trip as Clemens was for the *Alta*. The extent of her refining influence on his writing is evidenced by his telling another passenger, "Mrs Fairbanks has just destroyed another four hours' work for me", as well as by his reference to her, for the rest of her life, as "Mother Fairbanks".

A lifelong and even more demanding critic of his excesses was waiting in the wings. Another fellow-passenger was Charley Langdon, eighteen-year-old son of a wealthy coal factor in Elmira, New York State. Clemens's friendship with the young man led to his being shown, in the Bay of Smyrna, an ivory miniature of Langdon's sister, Olivia. With this the impressionable Clemens fell instantly in love, and when the *Quaker City* docked in New York he was introduced to this "sweet and timid and lovely young girl" in the hotel where the family was staying. He was even allowed to accompany them that evening to a reading by Charles Dickens, and the romance blossomed from that point.

persisted, while claiming that his advertisement of his first appearance – "Doors open at 7.30. The trouble will begin at 8" – was plaintive rather than facetious. It is more likely that this is an economy with the truth, a piece of mock-modesty introduced in the interests of maintaining the consistency of the diffident, insecure persona he has affected throughout the book. At this period of his life particularly, though, the insecurity was not wholly fictitious, but with what popularity and success he pursued this lecturing career to the end of his life will emerge later.

The less expected benefits came in the shape of three friends, all made on these trips. An American diplomat passing through Honolulu, Anson Burlinghame, was so impressed by him as to give him some advice that Clemens followed, if anything, almost too assiduously. Seeing in him great ability and potential genius, and taking a leaf out of Benjamin Franklin's book, Burlinghame told him: "What you need now is the refinement of association. Seek companionship among men of superior intellect and character. Refine yourself and your work. Never affiliate with inferiors; always climb."

On his trip to Europe Clemens was able to put this almost immediately into practice.

THE DESCENT OF VESUVIUS (bottom right) "was a labour of only four minutes". We "ploughed our way with prodigious strides that would almost have shamed the performance of him of the seven-league boots" (The Innocents Abroad).

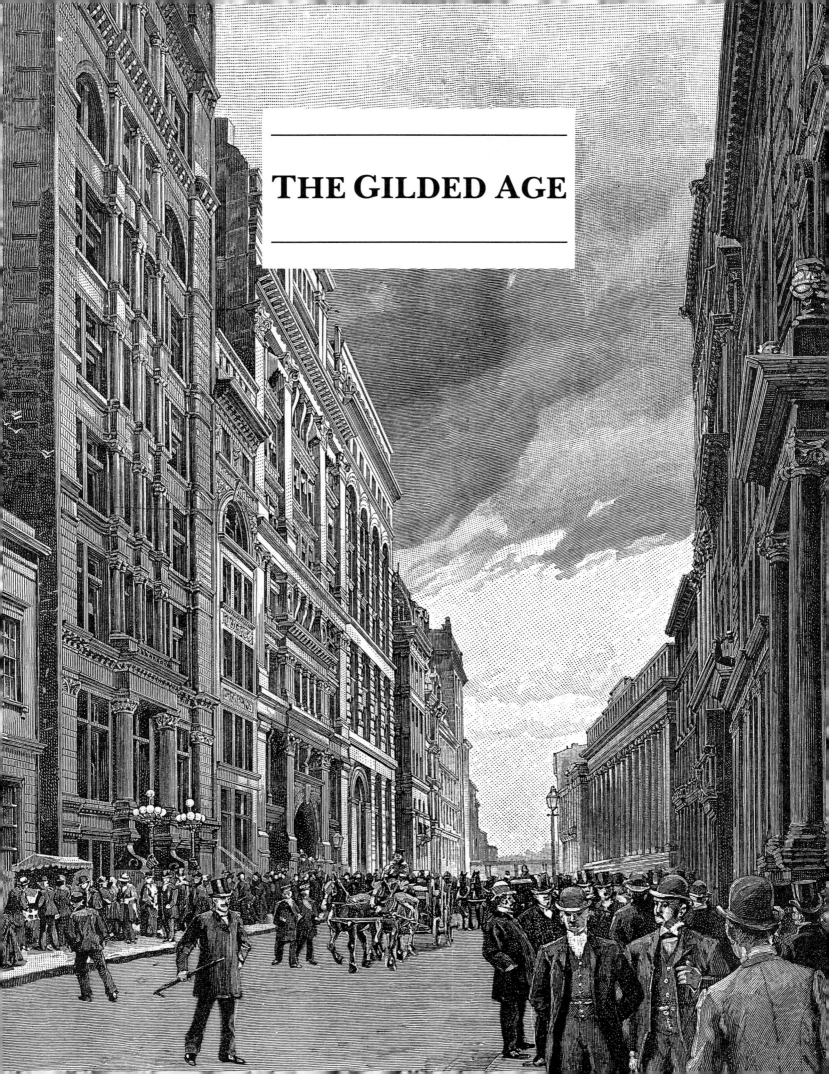

THE GILDED AGE

CHAPTER
3
MARK TWAIN AND THE EASTERN SEABOARD

It would be grossly unfair to suggest that Clemens's courtship of and eventual marriage to Olivia was in obedience to Burlinghame's advice, "Refine yourself . . . always climb". The romance of his first attraction to her appears to have lasted, the partnership to have been remarkably happy, and her death in Florence in 1903 to have deepened still further the bleak darkness of his own closing years. Whatever Charles Dickens made in cash from that New Year's Eve reading in 1867, Clemens always insisted that it was the evening on which he himself found "the fortune of my life". Nevertheless, aware that he needed to be a great deal more secure in a job before contemplating marriage, he did not see Olivia again until the summer. Journalism was too precarious and not respectable enough, especially as his postscript to the letters from the "Quaker City" trip, an article in the *New York Herald* roundly condemning the hypocrisy of the Pilgrims, threatened more notoriety than fame.

The Langdons were an eminently respectable, church-going family in Elmira, western New York State, where Olivia's

CENTRAL VIEW OF THE CITY OF NEW YORK, *1860 (opposite).* *Twain's letters home from the* Quaker City *had made him a celebrity, so that, when he returned to the USA, the New York* Tribune *invited him to join the staff. He had already acknowledged the importance of the city with the words, "Make your mark in New York, and you are a made man."*

father, Jervis Langdon, had made his wealth out of coal and iron. Their home was a specially designed brownstone mansion on Main Street in which their beautiful and only daughter would in any case have led a sheltered family life, but a spinal injury, suffered in a fall as a teenager, had for some years made a semi-invalid of her. For Clemens this doubtless heightened a desire to sustain the protection of such delicacy and increased the sense of his own unworthiness. The social difference between them would have been a source of uneasiness, as might the fact that Jervis had been an abolitionist; but even without Burlinghame, Clemens would have had ideas of upward mobility.

An appointment in Washington, D.C., as private secretary to James H. Stewart, senator for Nevada, lasted for two months before the two parted by mutual consent. The

THE CORNER OF BROAD AND WALL STREETS, NEW YORK *(above left). By the late 1860s, New York was the financial centre of the USA and set the trends in fashion and ideas that were followed by the whole nation. It was here that Twain first met Olivia Langdon, his future wife, and sister of a fellow voyager on the* Quaker City.

A NEW YORK DRINKING BAR *(left). The match between bohemian Twain and respectable Olivia seemed an unlikely one. She objected in particular to his drinking, smoking and bad language. During their courtship he therefore took the pledge, but was soon drinking again once they had married.*

OLIVIA IN 1869 *(right). Olivia Langdon had been brought up in Elmira, New York State. After injuring her spine in a fall at the age of 16, she remained delicate in health and led a very sheltered life. She and Twain were married in February 1870 after a formal engagement lasting one year, during which Twain wrote her nearly 200 letters.*

OLIVIA IN 1869 *(right). Olivia Langdon had been brought up in Elmira, New York State. After injuring her spine in a fall at the age of 16, she remained delicate in health and led a very sheltered life. She and Twain were married in February 1870 after a formal engagement lasting one year, during which Twain wrote her nearly 200 letters.*

SIXTH STREET WHARF, WASHINGTON, DC *(below), lithograph by Charles Magnus, 1863. During the autumn and winter of 1867–68, Twain worked for a short time in Washington as private secretary to James H. Stewart, senator for Nevada, but he was unhappy in the post and left after two months.*

success of a hastily-cobbled-together lecture and of his début as an after-dinner speaker, both in Washington, was followed by doubts as to whether the former was a career he wanted and the latter too racy to commend the reports of it to Mother Fairbanks and her like. His attempts at lobbying for an appointment in the public or the diplomatic service might have produced something, but he was not convinced that this was what he wanted; the political atmosphere of the time and the impeachment of President Andrew Johnson discouraged him from persevering.

The problem was compounded for him by an unsolicited approach from the Hartford publisher Elisha Bliss with the suggestion that the "Quaker City" letters, suitably revised, would make a book that he would be willing to publish. That Bliss's firm, the American Publishing Company, had one of the biggest markets for publishing by subscription was an added attraction. This method guaranteed quicker returns than the royalty system by means of large orders secured by travelling salesmen, and with down-payments in advance from the popular audience most likely to enjoy Mark

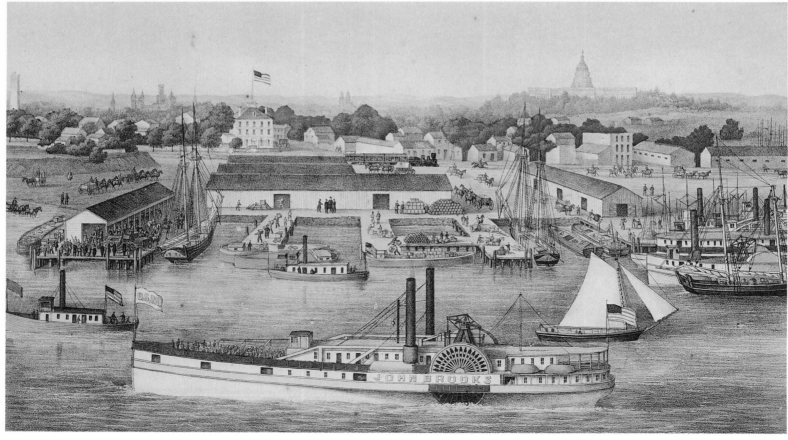

THE ROTUNDA AT WASHINGTON, DC *(left). Although he considered pursuing a diplomatic or political career in Washington, Twain was discouraged by the unsettled atmosphere. Following an attempt to gain control of the army by removing the Secretary of State for War, President Andrew Johnson had been impeached.*

THE CAPITOL, WASHINGTON, DC *(below left). Twain was later to satirize political life in* The Gilded Age.

at one sitting; a return visit to California, including some lecturing, also took place. That gave him the opportunity to persuade his old friend Bret Harte to read and advise him on the manuscript. Harte's suggested cuts and tonings-down were sweetened by his publishing in the *Overland Monthly* two chapters, after recommending their removal from the book. In August 1868 *The*

Twain's writings. That audience, though, demanded quantity for their money. Bliss stipulated six hundred pages: the letters to the *Alta California* amounted to less than half of that, and, in response to censure from his sister Pamela and Mrs Fairbanks, he had already undertaken to eradicate from them all vulgarity and "scoffing at sacred things". A formidable amount of new writing had to be accomplished, for there was also the fastidious but desirable Livy to impress.

The changes he made were less drastic than his correspondents might have wished, but his wisest decision was to eliminate the raffish "Mr Brown" whose role had lowered the tone of the letters, and to increase the significance of the persona of the narrator. The necessary 200,000 words were produced in eight weeks or so, sometimes 3,000

FRANCIS BRET HARTE (1836– 1902) *(left), humorist and novelist, was among the most important writers of fiction about the American West. When Twain returned to California in 1868 and began work on* The Innocents Abroad, *Harte read the original manuscript of the* Quaker City *correspondence and advised Twain about how to edit it. "It was a kind thing of Harte to do," wrote Twain, "and I think I appreciated it." Nevertheless, the relationship between the two men eventually deteriorated.*

Innocents Abroad was delivered to Bliss in Hartford and the relieved author went on to Elmira to a more welcome task.

His protestations of his strong wish to improve his character had the undesired effect of encouraging Olivia to urge a brother–sister relationship, with herself as the kindly reformer of the prodigal. In letters he continued his wooing, meeting refusals with as much patience as he could, and at last, in November, a triumphant lecture tour brought him back to Elmira as a more reputable public figure with a career of distinction opening up for him. Olivia's parents still needed more convincing than their daughter, but their misgivings are understandable, for the two seemed unlikely partners. One clue as to what finally convinced the Langdons is perhaps to be found in Olivia's lifelong term of endearment for Sam, "Youth". For all his rough, free, brash and bohemian manner, his capacity for enjoying life, his enthusiasms, his sense of wonder and surprise at what was always happening to him must have been as infectious as they were youthful.

Olivia, by contrast, was inexperienced, conventional in outlook, prim and so serious-minded that he had sometimes, in writing to her, to include an explanatory phrase such as "That is a joke, my literal Livy". Her principled hostility to alcohol, smoking, bad language and any other impropriety must have seemed to him at times insuperable, nor were his reiterated promises of reform implemented with any real dedication. This does not make them insincere: part of his boyishness was, no doubt, the persuasive conviction with which he argued the possibility of his fulfilling them. On Thanksgiving Day their engagement was approved, though not to be announced until the Langdons' enquiries about him were satisfactorily concluded. The opinion of Mrs Fairbanks as to his social and moral credentials, as well as his capacity for reform, was sought and received; others who were consulted were less reassuring. Matters hung in the balance, but on 4 February 1869 the engagement became official. They were married on 2 February 1870.

The ceremony took place at the parents' home in Elmira, and Clemens's autobiographical account describes the principal guests accompanying the newly-weds on the following day to Buffalo, where he was to

BUFFALO, NEW YORK STATE, 1873 *(below). Twain and his new bride moved here after their marriage, to a house given them as a wedding-present by the bride's father. Langdon also lent Twain money so that he could buy part-ownership of the Buffalo* Express.

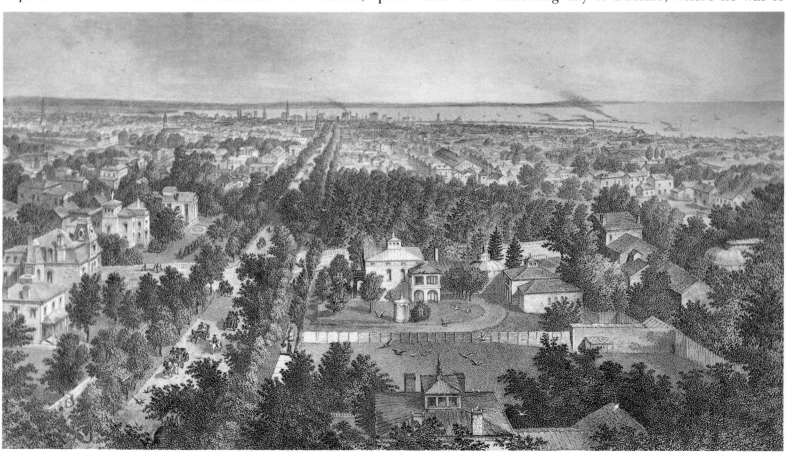

be part-owner and an editor of the *Express*. The journey from the railway station followed a circuitous route to the lodgings which he believed a friend had secured for them, only to terminate at premises which Clemens recognized to be well beyond his resources. This, however, was no boarding-house but Jervis Langdon's wedding present to him: a home of his own, fully furnished, staffed, and even with his own coach and coachman. The boy from Florida had walked into a fairy-tale.

There followed a thirty-four-year partnership with "the most perfect character I have ever met", of whom he was to say, after her death, "The love which she bestowed upon those whom she loved took the form of worship, and in that form it was returned – returned by relatives, friends and the servants of her household." For full measure also, "She was my faithful, judicious and painstaking editor" for "more than a third of a century". Her initiation into the mysteries of that craft had even preceded matrimony, for proofs of *The Innocents Abroad* arrived early in their engagement and they worked on them jointly.

Idyllic as his memories of it were, the marriage, like all others, was to have its tragedies. The first was not long in coming. Livy's father, shortly after the wedding, was fighting an illness which was found to be cancer. The young couple returned to Elmira to be with him and, although Olivia was already pregnant, to help care for him. When he died in August 1870 his distressed and exhausted daughter, whose health was never robust, had a breakdown through which her husband and her widowed mother nursed her in the Buffalo house.

Then in September a friend of Olivia's, on a visit to them, developed typhoid fever, was nursed by them in their home briefly, and died there. Small wonder that when, on 7 November, Livy gave birth prematurely to their son, Langdon, the baby was not strong; small wonder too that Mark Twain was falling increasingly behind schedule with the manuscript of *Roughing It*, due with Bliss by January, and was running into the first of the many "writer's blocks" that were to dog his career.

Had he not already, over-confident in his new-found wealth, abandoned the idea of lecturing in the 1870–1 season, his domestic problems would have prevented his fulfilling such engagements. Two or three humorous sketches were as much as his creative powers could accomplish, yet he needed money to support his mother and her family in Missouri, as well as his own family in New York State. His generous impulse in persuading Bliss to give his feckless brother Orion a job in the publishing

ORION CLEMENS AND HIS WIFE MOLLIE *(above left). It appears that Twain modelled the character of Washington Hawkins in* The Gilded Age *on his older brother Orion. A dreamer who pursued a variety of careers, all without much success, Orion was frequently supported by Twain.*

QUARRY FARM *(above right), near Elmira, summer home of Olivia's sister Mrs Crane, who built this special study a little way from the main house for Twain to write in. He continued to work here during the summers even after his spacious house in Hartford had been completed.*

HARTFORD, CONNECTICUT *(left). Twain took up residence in this thriving city in 1871 and built his own house there in 1874.*

house in Hartford was rebounding on him and adding to his problems. In desperation he sold up in Buffalo, and moved with his wife and son to her sister's summer home at Quarry Farm near Elmira. Here at least he could resume work on *Roughing It* at an increasing rate and with new confidence.

What he wanted most was to enable Livy to fulfil her ambition of setting up home in Hartford, an attractive city and by now one of America's wealthiest, as well as something of a cultural centre. At last, in the autumn of 1871, they were able to rent a house from friends in the Nook Farm area there and move in. Home ownership was not yet possible, for the initial impact of *The Innocents Abroad* was declining and *Roughing It,* which was urgently needed to reinstate his name and reputation, was not yet out. Ironically, and to his chagrin, the reputation of his one-time friend, Bret Harte, was vigorously (and, it seemed to Clemens, not wholly justifiably) in the ascendant. A return to the lecture platform that autumn brought some much-needed cash, advance publicity for the forthcoming book, and renewed public acclaim. It was bought, however, at a cost. Livy chafed at the long absences from home that the tours imposed on him, and the Eastern seaboard literati were not unanimous in their assessment of his creative originality. His self-esteem suffered from this and from his own sense of the social unworthiness of the "mere" humorist, although the support of a few writers, notably William Dean Howells, was to be a consolation.

So too was the closeness of the cultured Nook Farm community. The residents observed a happy informality of social visiting, congenial to the Clemenses, though often distracting to the literary concentration of Mark Twain. They were all people of some distinction, with two families predominating. These were the Hookers, descended from the seventeenth-century Congregationalist divine, Thomas Hooker, who had emigrated from England to Massachusetts in 1633, and the Beechers, whose father, Lyman, born a New Englander, became an eminent Presbyterian preacher on Long Island and later in Boston. In June 1869 Clemens had accompanied Olivia to the wedding in Hartford of her friend Alice Hooker, at which the officiating minister had been Lyman's son, Henry Ward Beecher; he, of course, should have been on the "Quaker City" excursion, and his brother Thomas was later to marry Clemens and Olivia in Elmira. Alice's mother was one of Henry's sisters, Isabella. She had married John Hooker, a lawyer, who had first developed the Nook Farm area; by 1871 she had only with difficulty come to accept Mark Twain socially, though it was the Hooker house they rented. Another of Lyman's daughters, better known by her married name of Harriet Beecher Stowe, also lived at Nook Farm with her husband,

MARK TWAIN WITH CHARLES DUDLEY WARNER *(left) fellow resident of the Nook Farm area. The two collaborated in writing* The Gilded Age, *an attempt to set a new standard in American fiction.*

Calvin Stowe, a scholar of significance in his own right, even if something of a prototype of the professor as popularly imagined. The record-breaking sales of her *Uncle Tom's Cabin,* published some twenty years earlier, Mark Twain was desperate to rival, but the two became good friends.

Nook Farm also contained two editors of the Hartford *Courant,* Joseph Hawley and Charles Dudley Warner, as well as his brother George Warner, whose wife, a second-generation Nook Farm resident, was the daughter of a United States senator. In all, it was distinguished and respectable company for a Missouri backwoodsman and failed silver prospector who, like his neighbours, quickly became sufficiently intimate with the Congregational minister, Joseph Hopkins Twichell, to know him as "Joe", as a friend, and as a kindred spirit.

By the end of 1871 prospects seemed better once more, and Olivia was pregnant again, but once more unforeseen disaster lay in wait. A daughter, Olivia Susan (Susy), was born on 19 March 1872. The ailing Langdon was ill at the time, but some weeks later, while recovering, he was allowed out for a drive in an open barouche, in his father's care. The morning was raw and cold, so Langdon was well wrapped up, but absent-mindedly Clemens failed to notice

AMERICAN HUMORISTS *(left), Mark Twain stands between Petroleum V. Nasby, pen-name of political satirist David Ross Locke (1833–88), and Josh Billings, pen-name of Henry Wheeler Shaw (1818–85), who specialized in deliberately misspelled cracker-barrel philosophy.*

him kick off the furs and expose his bare legs, so the baby caught a chill. "I was the cause of the child's illness", the grieving father convinced himself until the end of his life, but to Howells he once said, more dramatically, "*I* killed him", although it was of diphtheria that Langdon died on 2 June.

CLARA, JEAN AND SUSAN
CLEMENS, *(above), the three
daughters of Samuel and Olivia,
born in 1874, 1880 and 1872,
respectively. Only Clara, who
married the pianist Ossip
Gabrilowitsch, was to survive her
parents.*

aspirations to the newborn Susy. They were
to have two more daughters, Clara, born in
1874, and Jean, born six years later, but,
fond as their parents were of them both, it
was Susy to whom, until the 1890s, they
were primarily devoted.

Meanwhile life had somehow to be re-
sumed, and with the support of Nook Farm
friends and neighbours Clemens was able,
in the autumn of 1872 and alone, to pay the
first of the many visits to England that will
form the subject of much of Chapter 5.
With Olivia, her female companion and
Susy he was to return to Britain a few
months later in fulfilment of a spring programme of lecture engagements he had secured there. Before they left, however, the
dream of building their own home had
come nearer to fulfilment with the acquiring of a lot on Farmington Avenue and the
commissioning of Edward Tuckerman Potter, a New York architect with a reputation
for his church designs. Before they left,
Mark Twain completed another book, a
satiric novel written in collaboration with
his neighbour, Charles Dudley Warner.
The outcome of a typical Nook Farm dinner party conversation in which they and
their wives had agreed on the deplorable

The burden of guilt and self-reproach
was increasing once more on Clemens's
overloaded conscience, at the same time
that *Roughing It* was reviving his reputation
better than its sales were reviving his flagging fortunes. Langdon's death devastated
the couple and they understandably trans-
ferred immediately all their love, hopes and

SLEIGHING IN NEW YORK, 1855
*(right), lithograph by Thomas
Benecke. For wealthy Easterners
even the bitter cold of winter
could be enjoyable.*

state of American fiction, it was their attempt at setting a new standard.

The Gilded Age certainly proved a landmark, but hardly a revolution. Rather, the collaboration produced a sprawling, uncomfortable amalgamation of two stories, many loose ends, and an uneasy link through the sensational career of a beautiful *femme fatale*. Even though we do not know the division of labour in authoritative detail, Mark Twain's contributions are quickly identified by their lively originality, style and subject-matter. Warner, for example, could never have invented the major comic character, Colonel Beriah Sellers, whose role is unfortunately diminished as the novel progresses. Sellers seems a figure out of popular mythology until one realizes the extent to which the whole book must be seen as a *roman à clef*: even Sellers is drawn from Mark Twain's own acquaintance and heightened only slightly in the interest of comedy and topical satire.

The story opens in the ante-bellum South, with the impoverished Hawkins family deciding, like the Clemenses, on the desirability of removing from Tennessee to Missouri, confident that the land they own in Tennessee will one day bring them in a fortune. (Part of the Clemenses' family folklore had similarly centred on their own "Tennessee Land" that was to do the same for them. This superstition Sam abandoned long before more credulous relatives, though he was sometimes to joke that his income from *The Gilded Age* was the only revenue the Tennessee Land brought him.) The Hawkins family, on their journey west, adopt two more children, orphaned by an explosion on a riverboat which has placed too great a strain on its boilers by engaging in a race with another. This occurrence, not uncommon in river history, is graphically presented in the text. One of these orphans is Laura, who will become the link character already mentioned; the other, Clay, is one of the novel's loose ends, except as a contrast to Laura in his loyalty to the family. The fact of their adoption also proves less than crucial to the plot.

In Missouri "Judge" Hawkins renews his friendship with "Colonel" Sellers (both titles are purely honorific in the old Southern pattern) and these two incurable optimists buoy up each other's belief that vast spe-

THE FURNACE, IRON MOUNTAIN, MISSOURI (*above*). *The success of mining in Missouri made it a likely area for the kind of railroad speculation described in* The Gilded Age.

culative fortunes await them if only they can hit on the right project and sufficient capital simultaneously. Meanwhile the son, Washington Hawkins, is convinced that he can achieve success as an inventor. If the father is based on John Clemens, the naive Washington, who later becomes secretary to a senator in the national capital (as his author had done), is in all other respects unmistakably the author's brother Orion, while Sellers is modelled on Mark Twain's mother's Tennessee cousin, James Lampton, so clearly as to make the original instantly recognizable to a writer friend of Mark Twain who met him some years later.

Warner's narrative focuses on two young Easterners, Philip Sterling and Harry Brierly. Their eagerness for involvement in railroad development brings them to Missouri and into contact with Sellers, who persuades them into a scheme for bringing the track through land that he owns. Time has passed, and with it the Civil War; Judge Hawkins is dead, and Laura has been seduced into a bogus marriage with a Con-

THE COLONNADE OF A LARGE US HOTEL (*left*). *The pursuit of the leisured life of the wealthy was satirized in* The Gilded Age, *a title which came to sum up a whole period of American history.*

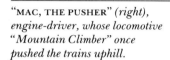

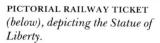

federate colonel who has later returned to his legal wife. Sellers's scheme for making Stone's Landing a major centre of communications depends on the development of a minor tributary of the Columbus River which needs only to be "widened, and deepened, and straightened, and made long enough" to turn it into "one of the finest rivers in the country". Readers attracted to the novel by Mark Twain's name and expecting characteristically ebullient comedy from so grandiose a scheme in the hands of such innocents are doomed to disappointment.

Sellers persuades not only the two young men but also the idealistic philanthropist Senator Dilworthy into lobbying for Congressional funds for this and also for the development of a university on the Tennessee land. All four of them, together with Washington Hawkins and Laura, whose femininity they all regard as a trump card in the game of persuading politicians, set off for Washington, D.C. An appropriation for the Stone's Landing scheme is secured and work is well underway before it is realized that the whole sum has been mortgaged in expenses, especially buying votes. The enterprise collapses, penniless; the route of the railway is deflected well away from Sellers's land, but, incapable of learning from experience, he remains confident of other successes.

As the scene shifts to Washington the main thrust of the novel becomes clear. Fiction becomes little more than a fig-leaf for naked fact. Senator Dilworthy's public-spirited and God-fearing adherence to pious and noble causes does not prevent his wheeling and dealing like all the rest, and his uplifting oratory is recognizably sanctimonious humbug. His eventual exposure for offering a bribe of $8,000 to a member of his state legislature, with a view to securing his own re-election, is identical, even down to the sum, to that of Samuel C. Pomeroy, Republican senator for Kansas, in January 1873. Fiction can hardly be more transparently topical, and even the illustrator's depiction of Dilworthy bore a strong resemblance to Pomeroy, whom Clemens had met during his short period as secretary to Senator Stewart.

The corruption of the administration of General Grant has now become a byword among historians, but it was this book that, to the embarrassment of many, brought it to the attention of the novel-reading public of its day. It might not unfairly be described as realistic rather than satiric in its relentless account of the machinations of public life and the power and methods of the lobbyists. The moral indignation of its authors is indisputable in their contempt for Washington as "the grand old benevolent National Asylum for the Helpless", much as Dickens had pilloried Parliament as "the national dust-heap".

Washington's social manners and customs are also satirized in Chapter 33, not much more gently, and Laura's cynical but constantly successful manipulation of men by her sexual attractiveness is clearly intended rather as a comment on the mores of the time than as the justifiable outcome of her embitterment at the Confederate

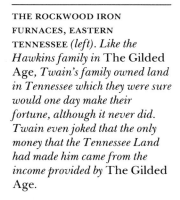

THE ROCKWOOD IRON FURNACES, EASTERN TENNESSEE *(left). Like the Hawkins family in* The Gilded Age, *Twain's family owned land in Tennessee which they were sure would one day make their fortune, although it never did. Twain even joked that the only money that the Tennessee Land had made him came from the income provided by* The Gilded Age.

colonel's heartless conduct. Even her downfall, it has been suggested, melodramatically engineered as it looks at first in fictional context, may have been based on the 1870 California case (with which Clemens is known to have been familiar) of a widow, Laura D. Fair. Like her fictitious counterpart, she too was tried for shooting her lover and acquitted on the grounds of "emotional insanity".

Warner and Mark Twain each wrote a version of the ending; their wives agreed in preferring the latter's, and so we have Laura's acquittal attributed to the dubious methods of lawyers, the unintelligence of jurors, and the malicious influence of the press. Any suggestion that the acquittal is a concession to the sentimental humanitarianism of readers who prefer a wronged heroine to survive is rebutted by a "twist in the tail" device. The narrative first con-

GENERAL ULYSSES S. GRANT (1822–1885) *(above), commander of the Union forces in the Civil War, and 18th president of the USA from 1969 to 1877.*

THE RECEPTION OF GENERAL GRANT AT PHILADELPHIA *(left). Although the corruption rife under Grant's administration was depicted in* The Gilded Age, *Twain's own publishing house later handled Grant's bestselling memoirs.*

PANIC AT THE SAN FRANCISCO
STOCK EXCHANGE (above). The
promise of riches summed up in
Colonel Sellers' constant cry,
"There's millions in it", had
infected the whole nation and
shameless speculation led to great
swings in economic stability.
Twain was himself affected by a
panic on Wall Street in 1873, the
year The Gilded Age was
published.

HARRIET BEECHER STOWE IN
OLD AGE, 1884 (right). The
Nook Farm community found
themselves divided by the scandal
surrounding Harriet's famous
brother, Henry Ward Beecher,
and his adulterous relationship
with a parishioner.

TWAIN PLAYING POOL (opposite
top) with the daugher of his
biographer, Albert Bigelow
Paine. Twain liked to relax by
playing billiards, and had a
billiard-room incorporated into
the design of his new house.

cludes the trial with her being gaoled for
life; then, arguing that "this is history and
not fiction", it introduces the "true" but
more cynical accounts of her release.

Her subsequent death from a heart attack
is moralistically attributed to her shameless
arrogance in aiming at a new career on the
lecture platform. A mere handful of people
attends her début, and their moral indignation impels them to drive her, unheard and
violently, out of the hall. The implications

that public taste is so moral as not to be
attracted by scandal, and that the audience's
violence against her is a justifiable manifestation of this, are two more of the book's
inconsistencies. The authors, however,
might not have been above citing its relatively disappointing sales to support the
former point.

Warner's contribution conforms more to
the clichés of the genteel fiction of the day:
Philip Sterling uncomplainingly meets the
debts incurred by Harry Brierly's extravagance, patiently and chivalrously woos the
Philadelphia Quaker, Ruth Bolton (whose
pursuit of a medical career recognizes the
incipient contemporary feminism) and
eventually repays her father's faith in him
by striking a rich vein of coal in the mine in
which they have both invested. Eli Bolton
himself is the generous victim of fraudulent
speculators; his sacrifice of the family
home, rather than fail his creditors, foreshadows with unforeseeable irony Mark
Twain's later life. It also contrasts markedly
with the credit ethos of the age as epito-
mized in the quotation, unattributed by the
authors to any specific person: "I wasn't
worth a cent two years ago, and now I owe
two millions of dollars."

The Gilded Age, as reviewers on both sides
of the Atlantic lost no time in suggesting, is
diffuse and ill-constructed, its political satire uncomfortably like washing dirty linen
in public (before an international public,
too), and the epigraphs to every chapter,
selected for the authors by a Hartford scholar from texts in languages ranging from
Old Norse to Sioux-Dakota, are preten-
tiously recondite. (Only in a later edition
did an appendix provide translations.)
Henry Adams's Democracy was to provide in
1880 a more influential and sophisticated
attack on corruption in the capital. Mark
Twain's dramatization of The Gilded Age for
the stage, though, proved very popular
and, as Colonel Sellers, John T. Raymond
increased his theatrical reputation significantly. Later Clemens and Howells collaborated on Colonel Sellers as a Scientist, a play
that did not enjoy the same success.

Social historians immediately adopted the
title, The Gilded Age, to give that whole
period of American history a peculiarly apt
and memorable name, highlighting its
affluence at the same time as calling into

as the covered balcony opening off it resembled the boat's Texas-deck.

Another oddity may have been suggested by the Reform Club in London, where Charles Barry had incorporated such a feature in 1837: this was the window immediately above the dining-room fireplace that gave the impression in winter of snowflakes falling directly into the fire. The library fireplace was imported from Ayton Castle near Edinburgh, an L-shaped divan

question the solidity of the foundations of that wealth. In the year of its publication, 1873, Clemens, in England with his family, had the doubtful pleasure of seeing his scepticism vindicated when a panic on Wall Street lost him and Olivia a considerable fortune. It even prevented them from contributing, as they wished, to the fund for installing an American window in Shakespeare's church in Stratford-upon-Avon. At the same time the new house in Hartford was nearing completion, and at least they were able to occupy that in 1874.

The house constitutes in itself an embodiment of the Gilded Age as well as of the tastes of its owners. Restored now to most of its original glory as the Mark Twain Memorial, it contributes vividly to an understanding of Clemens's personality as a man and as a writer. The idiosyncratic red-brick exterior is sometimes spoken of as in the English style, but it is much more eclectic than that implies. In speaking of "the novelty displayed in the architecture . . . and the oddity of its internal arrangements" the *Hartford Daily Times* of the day was nearer the mark. One of these oddities is to be expected: a circular wall in an upstairs dressing-room seems intended to evoke the pilot house of a Mississippi riverboat, much

DRAWING-ROOM OF MARK TWAIN'S HOUSE *(below left)*, at number 351 Farmington Avenue, Hartford. Now preserved as the Mark Twain Memorial, the house that he commissioned architect Edward Tuckerman Potter to design was itself a monument to Twain's gilded age. It had nineteen principal rooms and was so expensive to run that from time to time the family had to move to Europe to economize for a while.

THE DINING-ROOM *(centre left)* with its window above the fireplace, which may have been suggested by a similar feature in the Reform Club in London.

MAHOGANY GUEST ROOM *(below)* containing original bed and dresser.

in the study was modelled on one Clemens remembered in a Syrian monastery, and the great carved bed had been acquired in Venice. On this he slept regularly with his head at the foot so as to awaken facing the carved angels at the head. Folding doors separated the library from the dining-room; when opened, these enabled up to eighty people to watch the amateur theatricals in which the family delighted as much as their Nook Farm friends. A semicircular conservatory adopted a design popularized by Harriet Beecher Stowe, who, in absent-minded old age, frequently wandered into the house to play the piano. A fountain, vines, and plants set directly into the ground gave the conservatory its character. Upstairs, a billiard room was indispensable to Clemens's relaxation, even though it had to double as a workplace for him when the study became the children's classroom for some time.

In 1881 the house was redecorated by Louis Comfort Tiffany, whose stencilled wallpapers and other innovations have been as far as possible faithfully reproduced and replaced in the present-day Memorial. An additional strip of land was acquired, and by then the total expenditure on land, house and furnishings totalled $131,000, a sizeable sum even by the standards of the Gilded Age. Though not to everyone's taste, it was a house typical of its period, a piece of conspicuous consumption of which that period's most popular critic was inordinately, if illogically, proud.

DINING-ROOM (right) before Tiffany decor. As part of extensive refurbishments and extensions carried out in 1881, Twain arranged for the house to be redecorated by Louis Comfort Tiffany, leading American interior designer of his day and now more widely known for his hand-made iridescent glass.

THE LIBRARY (right) after Tiffany had redecorated in 1881. The luxurious conservatory adjoining the library was heated to provide flowers throughout the winter and boasted a permanent fountain.

TOM SAWYER
LIFE ON THE MISSISSIPPI
HUCKLEBERRY FINN
PUDD'NHEAD WILSON

MARK TWAIN AND THE OLD SOUTH

House-proud as Clemens undeniably was, his wife's observation that he seemed "to glory in his sense of possession" may be applied to more than that at this time. The quality and quantity of the work he was to produce in the next few years suggest an increasing confidence in his possession of craftsmanship and purpose, as well as self-possession. This was not, perhaps, to be expected after *The Gilded Age*. Disappointment at its reception reinforced the disillusion built into the story: however vigorously its Preface proclaimed his "great strong faith in a noble future for my country", the story's emphasis on the acquisitiveness of the age and the corruption of American political life belied it. The happiness of his domestic life, however, offset political cynicism, and although he retreated once more into retrospection, this time it was towards what his friend Howells once spoke of as the rightful subject for the novelist, "the smiling aspects of life, which are the more American". Certainly no one had more faith in his friend's next book than Howells.

The book, of course, was *The Adventures of Tom Sawyer*. This time "the wild humorist of

OLD KENTUCKY HOME LIFE IN THE SOUTH, 1859 (opposite), a detail of the picture by Eastman J. Johnson (1824–1906). Painted only two years before the Civil War, this idyllic view of plantation life is thought to have been intended as part of the pro-slavery propaganda to counter the impact of Uncle Tom's Cabin *in 1852.*

WILLIAM DEAN HOWELLS *(above), editor of* Atlantic Monthly *and a close friend of Twain, described* Tom Sawyer *as "Altogether the best boy's story I ever read", and predicted "It will be an immense success".*

OLIVIA AND THE CHILDREN, *1884 (left). Twain's three daughters were educated by their mother and a governess until they were old enough to attend the Hartford Public High School.*

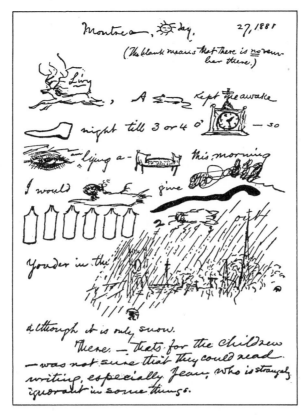

the Pacific slope", as he had become known, was to go back beyond the persona that had made him famous: he was no longer writing as the rough product of the mining frontier, the irresponsible bachelor who had no ties of family or class to inhibit his irreverence, and who, when visiting Europe, had prided himself on being "one of the boys". When Howells described *Tom Sawyer* as "altogether the best boy's story I ever read",

it was not that kind of boy that he had in mind. Its author was now a family man with a reputation as a writer, lecturer and wit, even in the Europe he had earlier mocked. Delightful as the book is, not enough of the earlier boy survived in him to resist successfully the efforts of his wife and Howells to bring the first draft more into line with the genteel tradition of the day. Even so, too much must not be made of the modifications his mentors suggested: Tom remains the quintessentially mischievous boy in a small Mississippi riverside town strikingly like Hannibal, even if it is called St. Petersburg. Again it is on some of Mark Twain's own acquaintances that many characters are based, and again there is no great distance between fiction and autobiography.

The upbringing of Tom (and his brother Sid) is in the hands of good-natured Aunt Polly. Her common sense is not always a match for his ability to get himself into scrapes or his engaging ingenuity in talking himself out of them, as in the celebrated scene where, set to paint a fence as punishment, he inveigles his friends into doing it for him. Becky Thatcher, his sweetheart, questions the extent of his devotion to her, so yet once more he plays hooky and engages in a series of boyish adventures. On a nocturnal visit to a graveyard with his disreputable comrade, Huck Finn, son of a ne'er-do-well father, he witnesses the murder of the local doctor by Injun Joe and the villain's attempt to incriminate the innocent, though intoxicated, Muff Potter. On another escapade they hide out on an island in the river, are presumed drowned, but return in time to attend the funeral service held for them. Tom's evidence, at Muff's

once. He did not know that it would constitute for him one of the most formidable cases of writer's block in his career.

A debate between Howells and Clemens as to whether *Tom Sawyer* should be issued as specifically for children was resolved by Mark Twain's admission in the Preface that although writing "mainly for the entertainment of boys and girls", he had hoped also "to pleasantly remind adults of what they once were themselves". Certainly the book is the antithesis of the hundred and thirty didactically "improving" books that Horatio Alger was so successfully inflicting on American boys of the time. Alger's young heroes also found a monetary reward awaiting them at the end of their adventures, but they had not had so much fun on the way to it as the boys of St Petersburg, and their moral virtues had, in the process, been more rigorously tempted than Tom's.

Mark Twain's benevolent perspective on childhood is essentially the adult's. We are never encouraged to take with any seriousness the threat of Injun Joe and the other villains. The agonies of Tom's calf-love for Becky are more distressing to the boy than to the reader. Tom's affection for her is expressed purely protectively, both in the cave and earlier, when he has nobly taken the punishment that should have been hers for accidentally tearing the teacher's book. This book, at which childish curiosity has

TOM SAWYER (left). Aunt Polly sets Tom to whitewashing the fence in the 1973 United Artists/ Reader's Digest film Tom Sawyer, *directed by Don Taylor.*

trial, restores his reputation. Then he and Becky, on a school picnic, get lost for some days in a cave. Here a chance glimpse of Injun Joe, still at large, heightens Tom's sense of his own danger but he finds a way out of the cave for himself and Becky.

Mark Twain's strength as a writer of anecdotes, evident in his earlier books, is well utilized in the opening chapters of *Tom Sawyer*, but after Chapter 6 the devising and sustaining of even a simple story-line gives him rather more difficulty. It has been pointed out that the happy ending, demanded by both convention and artistic consistency, is provided in a form somewhat ambivalent in the context: Injun Joe's hidden treasure, discovered by Tom and Huck, is divided between them, but the adults invest it in a trust fund for the boys that earns six per cent – a solution likely to be more acceptable to the Gilded Age than to two youngsters who prefer playing pirates. This "simply prodigious" income imposes on the two a respectability which Huck's spirited independence, after three weeks, cannot tolerate. His contracting out of it at least suggested to his creator the idea of following Huck's own adventures in a further book, which he began almost at

TOM SAWYER MALINGERS (below), in a scene from the 1930 film directed by John Cromwell.

BECKY THATCHER (*below left*), "*a lovely little blue-eyed creature with yellow hair plaited into two long tails*", *from the 1973 film version of* Tom Sawyer *produced by United Artists/ Reader's Digest.*

ORIGINAL MANUSCRIPT OF *TOM SAWYER* (*below right*): *half way through writing the book Twain felt his* "*tank had run dry*" *and put it aside to be completed two years later.*

led her to sneak a glance, turns out to be an anatomical work, and she is looking at "a handsomely engraved and colored frontispiece – a human figure, stark naked". Howells is sometimes accused of humourless prudery for his marginal note on the manuscript, "I should be afraid of this picture incident", yet his criticism may have been based on literary grounds: the situation requires only that the book be one which the teacher usually keeps locked away, and the hint, however faint, of nascent sexuality on Becky's part jars with the otherwise idyllic note of innocence pervading the novel. This is a world safe for children, its threats to them more apparent than real, the kind of world attractive to the hopes of young parents (as the Clemenses were), and as such it still holds its delight. Its fun is recognizably human, down-to-earth, and the Southern never-never land in which it is set is more satisfying than Barrie's in *Peter Pan* with its fey, whimsical atmosphere of wish-fulfilment.

Once he had finished a book Mark Twain's interest in it diminished rapidly. The insistence of Olivia and Howells detained him longer than he wished over corrections to *Tom Sawyer*; domesticity, social activities, quarrels with the Beechers, the trial of Henry Ward Beecher on adultery charges, problems with Orion, closer but fluctuating relations with Bret Harte (both personal and professional), combined with his own enthusiasm for investing in usually ill-conceived inventions by others – all these distractions, in the mid-1870s, and more, disturbed his concentration on the numerous literary projects occupying his mind simultaneously. The summer escapes to Quarry Farm offered the best opportunity for uninterrupted creative work. Yet somehow, by the end of 1875, *Tom Sawyer* was with the American publishers and on its

home town. Ironically, the English edition was on sale six months before the American, and by the time Bliss had been galvanized into action, not only had copious extracts appeared in the American newspapers but 100,000 copies had flooded the States from Canada, to the understandable fury of the author. He estimated that this piracy lost him $10,000; it also consolidated for the rest of his life his already considerable personal hostility to, and profound mistrust of, Elisha Bliss.

It fed another animosity. He had induced Harte (now also resident in Hartford) to publish with them, and Harte, with whose business Bliss was equally negligent, felt that Clemens should intercede on his behalf and meanwhile subsidize him generously with loans. Rather like Hawkins and Sellers, they began to dream up schemes for making a quick fortune jointly, and seeing the theatre as an appropriate territory, collaborated on a comedy. The formula seemed promising; it was to be set in the mining area of California which both knew intimately, it would capitalize on the popularity of Harte's poem "The Heathen Chinee" by appropriating its main character, Ah Sin,

way to the British, a collection of *Sketches, New and Old* had appeared, the *Atlantic Monthly* had published a major series of his reminiscences of the Mississippi, and other ideas were developing.

It will be seen in the next chapter how important a watershed in his international reputation the London edition of *Tom Sawyer* would become, but in the excitement of negotiating the arrangements for that Clemens characteristically neglected to watch Bliss's progress with the book in his

as its eponymous hero, and it would borrow from *Roughing It* the character of Scotty Briggs, already established in the popular imagination. Hard-pressed financially, Harte was capable of working prodigiously and with a flair that Clemens could envy more readily than emulate. Harte's earlier kindness to him, when he was starting as a novice in San Francisco, he could not ignore, and he had a genuine respect for Harte's expert craftsmanship. Though a year younger, Harte had begun his literary career earlier, and his reputation intensified the ambivalence of Mark Twain's attitude towards him.

All this did not augur well for the partnership. In the summer of 1877 *Ah Sin* opened indifferently in Washington and went on to disaster in New York. Dictating his memoirs thirty years later, Clemens had still not forgiven Harte for his casualness in business matters and especially for his debts, which *Ah Sin* had done nothing to pay off. He recalled that when the debt to him reached $3,000, Harte offered him his note, "but I was not keeping a museum and didn't take it". There is evidence, however, that he actually proposed another theatrical collaboration to Harte at the time, but that it was Harte who, no doubt wisely, turned down the offer. Mark Twain's next venture, *The Prince and the Pauper*, begun in November 1877, is better discussed later in this narrative, given its English historical theme and setting.

It is kinder, too, not to dwell on the unfortunate flight of fancy with which he responded to the invitation to speak at the seventieth birthday dinner for the Quaker poet, John Greenleaf Whittier, in Boston the following month. This compliment by the Boston literary establishment prompted him, over-boldly, to revert to the role of the "wild humorist of the Pacific slope" with an invented Western anecdote involving the three most venerable American writers of the day, Ralph Waldo Emerson, Oliver Wendell Holmes and Henry Wadsworth Longfellow. All were in or near their seventies, and all were in his audience, as were many other influential men of letters including Howells, who was to refer to the speech memorably as "that hideous mistake of poor Clemens's". It was irreverently tasteless rather than offensive, and its impact was less disastrous than has been represented, less damaging too than its conscience-stricken perpetrator always believed, but he characteristically never forgave himself.

In April 1878 he escaped from these disasters to Europe, this time with his wife, two daughters, and a small retinue, soon to be augmented, at Clemens's expense, by Joe Twichell, less as a spiritual mentor than as a

OLD KENTUCKY HOME LIFE IN THE SOUTH, 1859 (left), by Eastman J. Johnson. (1824–1906). Significantly, segregation is played down and racial harmony suggested by the Southern belle benignly, if cautiously, visiting the attractive slave quarters. Twain does not idealise in this way.

walking companion. Twichell had suggested to him, on a long walk in Connecticut, the desirability of writing up for publication the memories of Mississippi piloting with which he had been regaling the minister: it may be that Clemens hoped for a similar stimulus on this trip. Their tour, and the writings it produced, are again better deferred for later consideration. In September Clemens, now grey-haired, took the family back to an America to which, after an even longer escape to Europe, the former president, General Grant, had also returned with his.

Invited to make one of the speeches at a Chicago banquet in Grant's honour in November, Mark Twain wisely spoke as the author of *Tom Sawyer*, a family man paying a light-hearted tribute to childhood as the father of manhood. Adroitly he managed to intersperse some edged comments more appropriate to *The Gilded Age*, prompting the large and very varied audience to an enthusiasm particularly gratifying to him after the Boston disaster. He may have been encouraged by the recollection of the success of a speech he had given at a similarly patriotic dinner in Hartford in 1877, when he had reminisced publicly for the first time on his own inglorious military career. What was to become in 1885 "The Private History of a Campaign that Failed" had its genesis

that night, but if those adventures were in his mind in Chicago, it was due less to meeting again the victor of the Civil War than to the preoccupation with the Old South that still obsessed him.

The articles that he had written for the *Atlantic* in 1875 had been collectively entitled "Old Times on the Mississippi"; they had exhausted neither his memories of, nor his interest in, the topic. Writing *Tom Sawyer* and beginning *Huckleberry Finn* had revived them, and although he followed *The Prince*

and the Pauper with *A Tramp Abroad* in 1880, his imagination was still in the South. Attractive as was the idea of being trapped permanently in a boyhood in Tom Sawyer's world, the dream of being permanently a riverboat pilot had at least an equal allure.

MARKET SCENE (right), showing woman selling live chickens.

"A WATER-MELON FEAST" (below). Twain sought to convey the flavour of life in the Old South in Life on the Mississippi.

His own extravagant Hartford lifestyle, augmented by Orion's continuing requests for financial backing for new hare-brained schemes, led Clemens inevitably into further unwise speculations, and money again became an all-consuming problem. He began editing a *Library of Humour* in the conviction that it would be a money-spinner, made Charles L. Webster, a nephew of twenty-eight his business manager, and on the death of Elisha Bliss in 1880, decided to publish in future with James R. Osgood of Boston, despite Osgood's indifferent track record. Starts on other literary projects proving abortive, the temptation to travel prevailed once more, and in 1882 he returned for the first time in twenty-one years to his roots in the South, accompanied by Osgood and a secretary.

They travelled, naturally, by steamboat from St Louis to New Orleans, where the meeting of the three best-known Southern writers of the day marked for Clemens a highlight of the trip: Mark Twain was at last in the company of Joel Chandler Harris, whose stories had been brought together in *Uncle Remus: His Songs and His Sayings* in the previous year, and George Washington Cable, already the author of *Old Creole Days* (1879), *The Grandissimes* (1880) and *Madame*

ADVERTISEMENT FOR WILLIAMANTIC SIX CORD SPOOL COTTON (right), with the steam boats that carried cotton cargoes to the coast.

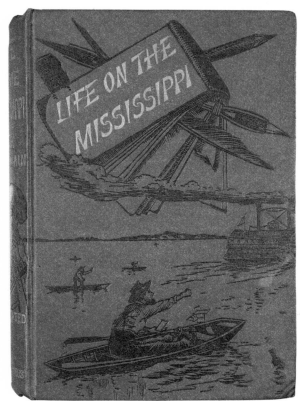

STREET SCENE IN NEW ORLEANS (left): "A middle-aged negro woman projected her head through a broken pane and shouted (very willing that the neighbors should hear and envy), 'You Mary Ann, come in de house dis minute!'" (Life on the Mississippi).

Delphine (1881), who would continue writing for almost a quarter of a century. Both were younger than Clemens, but the three revelled in each other's company. In other respects, however, the trip was a disappointment to the returned expatriate, for the Old South had changed beyond recognition, yet in one sense that fact acted as a new spur to his creative imagination.

He returned to Hartford to a prolonged period of recurrent illness among all members of the family, but he was determined to make a book (and some money) out of this latest journey as he had out of the others. He had, after all, the seven *Atlantic* articles, so far uncollected, as a nucleus; to these could be added his latest impressions of the New South. As *Life on the Mississippi*, this was published by Osgood in 1883.

The book opens with a two-chapter description of the river and its history, in which factual information is deployed vividly and stimulatingly. To the foreigner especially, the opening paragraph's disclosure that the Mississippi's drainage basin alone is "as great as the combined areas of England, Wales, Scotland, Ireland, France, Spain, Portugal, Germany, Austria, Italy and Turkey" can still be revelatory. To the American, the eclectic list of historical events that have taken place since the river was first

LIFE ON THE MISSISSIPPI (right): "The parting chorus" watches the steamer winging its way up the river.

"THE WASP" *(opposite left),* oversees the loading of fuel onto the river steamer.

LIFE ON THE MISSISSIPPI (right): "The parting chorus" watches the steamer winging its way up the river.

"THE WASP" *(opposite left),* oversees the loading of fuel onto the river steamer.

LIFE ON THE MISSISSIPPI (below): "We began to cool off."

THE STEAMER "GREAT REPUBLIC" *(below right), a typical river boat with her* "two tall, fancy-topped chimneys" *(Life on the Mississippi).*

seen by a white man, De Soto, in 1542, can be as novel as the statement that, after 1542, "for a century and a half the Mississippi remained out of the market and undisturbed" as "nobody needed it, nobody was curious about it".

Mark Twain's use of statistics in this book is generally less perfunctory and more idiosyncratic than in some of his nonfiction. There is, for example, the casual comment on the growth of one riverside town – "The first time I ever saw St Louis, I could have bought it for six million dollars, and it was the mistake of my life that I did not do it" – as well as the sustained excursion into data more exact than, he claims, geology can usually argue from:

In the space of one hundred and seventy-six years the Lower Mississippi has shortened itself two hundred and forty-two miles. That is an average of a trifle over one mile and a third per year. Therefore, any calm person, who is not blind or idiotic, can see that in the Old Oolitic Silurian period, just a million years ago next November, the Lower Mississippi River was upwards of one million three hundred thousand miles long, and stuck out over the Gulf of Mexico like a fishing-rod.

His generalized deduction from this has a splendidly mock-Franklinian ring: "There is something fascinating about science. One gets such wholesale returns of conjecture out of such a trifling investment of fact."

Chapter 3 continues the history by the disingenuous introduction of a lengthy excerpt "from a book which I have been working at, by fits and starts, during the past five or six years, and may possibly finish in the course of five or six more". His estimate is pessimistic: *The Adventures of Huckleberry Finn* was complete in less than two, though it did not repeat this chapter in which Huck overhears a party of thirteen men carousing on a raft (as in the genre painting of George Caleb Bingham) and outdoing each other with the wild boasts of the frontiersmen of folk tales.

The most satisfying section of the book now follows, the *Atlantic* essays, in which Clemens relives his days training to be a

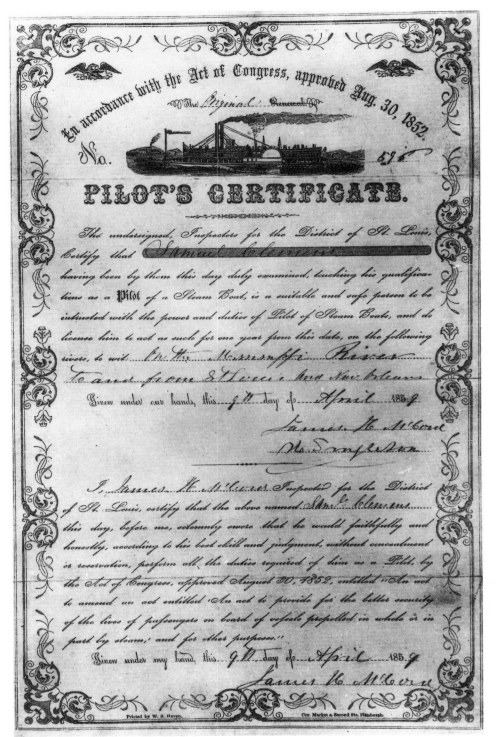

Mississippi pilot in a plangent, evocative piece of writing that must rank among his best for its sensitive combination of disciplined humour, nostalgia and genuine feeling, as well as for its re-creation of riverscape and atmosphere. One statement at the beginning of Chapter 14 has a particular resonance, when he explains why he "took a measureless pride" in the pilot's profession, loving it "far better than any I have followed since": "The reason is plain: a pilot, in those days, was the only unfettered and entirely independent human being that lived in the earth."

That this parallels his admiration for Judge Oliver in *The Innocents Abroad* is apparent from his account of Horace Bixby, the thirty-four-year-old pilot who "learned him the river". More irascible than the judge, Mr Bixby can be highly and vocally critical of the inadequacies of his apprentice, but the cub pilot already knows that his master "only carried just so many rounds of ammunition, and was sure to subside into a very placable old smallbore as soon as they were all gone". So, having "fine inspirations of prudence in those days", the lad (who is appalled at the details of the twelve hundred miles of river he is expected to know intimately in both directions and by night as well as by day) already knows, instinctively, enough about people to hold his peace until Bixby is "out of adjectives". Yet Bixby's self-control in an emergency and his quietly gentle, patient correction of his pupil's errors, when they arise from inexperience and not from inattention, are equivalent to Judge Oliver's. The lesson that "A pilot must have a memory but . . . he must have good and quick judgment and decision, and a cool, calm courage that no peril can shake" is a lesson for life, not merely for piloting, and one that Clemens constantly restates in different forms and contexts.

RIVER PILOT'S CERTIFICATE *(above). Trained by Horace Bixby, Twain received his license as Pilot of steam boats in 1859 and served as a steersman until the Civil War halted river traffic. "Piloting on the Mississippi River was not work to me; it was play" (Autobiography).*

MIDNIGHT RACE ON THE
MISSISSIPPI (right), lithograph by
Currier and Ives, c. 1866. "The
public always had an idea that
racing was dangerous; whereas
the very opposite was the case"
(Life on the Mississippi).
However, the riverboat explosion
at the beginning of The Gilded
Age (suggested by the death of
Twain's younger brother,
Henry), may have helped to form
the public's idea of the dangers of
racing.

CYPRESS SWAMP NEAR THE
MISSISSIPPI (right): "one could
believe that human creatures had
never intruded there before"
(Life on the Mississippi).

SICILIAN FRUITSELLER (above),
one of the traders lining the banks
of the Mississippi.

His navigational skills, his expert knowledge of the river and his confident ability to negotiate its hazards without jeopardizing his craft, as well as the unquestioning deference shown him by other pilots and even the captains, mark Bixby incontrovertibly as a professional. It is this professionalism that commands Clemens's respect, and that he learns assiduously to emulate as a pilot, acquiring in the process a self-respect that he seems not to have found in any other vocation. Nevertheless, it revolutionizes his attitude to the river in a way that he is realistic enough to recognize and accept: "I had lost something that could never be restored to me while I lived. All the grace, the beauty, the poetry had gone out of the majestic river!" If he re-learnt that lesson when he returned to the river in 1882, he was at least able, in the persona of young Huck Finn, to re-create imaginatively, for future generations, something of that grace, beauty and poetry he had known on the river of his youth.

The consistency with which he maintains in those chapters the point of view of the awed but keen cub pilot gives them a sharpness of focus that is quickly dissipated when he describes his more recent return to the South. The point of view of a man in his forties is likely to be more complex, but the

material is more diffuse and less well integrated: not for the first time does the reader feel that Mark Twain's freshness of enthusiasm for a subject can too quickly evaporate in the discipline of working it up

RIVER LIFE *(left):* "*At high water, the juvenile population perches on the beams of the wharves, and enjoys a little quiet fishing.*"

into a book of predetermined length in a given time. We have no record of his conversation with Anthony Trollope in England in the 1870s, but in that decade the Englishman was writing his *Autobiography* (it was published posthumously in the same year as *Life on the Mississippi*), and on at least two literary principles, enunciated there with unusual candour, Mark Twain would certainly have agreed. One was that the most essential piece of an author's equipment was some cobbler's wax to keep him fastened to his chair daily until he had completed the number of words required to meet his deadline. (Clemens would have needed more of this commodity than the less mercurial Trollope.) Second, if an author's material does not extend to the desired length, it must be padded or otherwise spun out until it does; that stratagem Mark Twain too often employs far more obviously than Trollope. In the text and appendices of this book, for example, whole pages are lifted (though always with acknowledgement) from newspapers and other authors such as Captain Marryat, and much is self-admitted gossip, however lively the anecdotes and the descriptive vignettes.

Disillusioned as he was with the New South, he tries to recognize its adjustment to its new circumstances, its manufactures, industrialization and other signs of progress. He carries his return journey on the river up to Minnesota, where it rises, thus bringing to an end "one of the most enjoyable five-thousand-mile journeys I have ever had the good fortune to make" – a judgment strangely at variance with the impression given in his letters home, and with his reference to "this wretched God-damned book" as it was going through the press. These epithets might apply to the South as he presents it.

He concludes, as he began, with mock statistics, this time of the twin cities of Minneapolis and St Paul:

When I was born, St Paul had a population of three persons, Minneapolis had just one third as many. The then population of Minneapolis died two years ago; and when he died he had seen himself undergo an

A PLANTER'S HOME ON THE MISSISSIPPI RIVER *(left), by unknown artist. Note the steamboat in the distance.*

SIR WALTER SCOTT'S WRITING TABLE AND CHAIR *(above left), at his home in Abbotsford.*

SIR WALTER SCOTT *(above right): Twain blamed what he called "the Sir Walter disease" of nostalgically romanticizing the past for the inability of the Southern states to compete in the late nineteenth-century commercial world.*

increase, in forty years, of fifty-nine thousand nine hundred and ninety-nine persons. He had a frog's fertility.

Yet the people of this "great and populous North-west . . . compel homage" from him as their Southern contemporaries manifestly do not. The Northerners are "an independent race who think for themselves, and who are competent to do it, because they are educated and enlightened".

This panegyric – and there is more of it – in Chapter 58 is best understood if it is juxtaposed with Chapter 46, "Enchantment and Enchanters", which contains the much-quoted diatribe against the influence of Sir Walter Scott "with his enchantments":

the sillinesses and emptinesses, sham grandeurs, sham gauds, and sham chivalries of a brainless and worthless long-vanished society. He did measureless harm; more real and lasting harm, perhaps, than any other individual that ever wrote. Most of the world has now outlived good part of these harms, though by no means all of them; but in our South they flourish pretty forcefully still . . . But for the Sir Walter disease, the character of the Southerner . . . would be

wholly modern, in place of modern and medieval mixed, and the South would be fully a generation further advanced than it is.

Culminating as it does in the suggestion that Scott is "in great measure responsible" for the Civil War, this attack can be too readily dismissed as typical Twainian leg-pulling hyperbole: the thesis is far more deeply-felt, far more tenable than that, in its encapsulation of this regenerated Southerner's courageous charge that the region is so unable to stop discussing the war, so committed to retrospect, so drenched in nostalgia for the moonlight and magnolias of a romanticized, chivalrous past, as to be incapable of surviving by competition in the cut-throat commercialism of a contemporary world. To suggest he is contradicting himself by apparently endorsing here the business ethic he had condemned in *The Gilded Age* is to invite a rejoinder like Whitman's, "Very well: I contradict myself"; to foresee that he will be inconsistent again when he writes *A Connecticut Yankee in King Arthur's Court* would have produced from Mark Twain a response as explosive as Emerson's notebook entry, "Damn consistency!" For all the indignant exaggeration of its expression, Mark Twain makes a fundamentally serious point in this chapter.

For his progress as a writer the trip was beneficial in another way too. Revisiting Hannibal, changed as the town was, "convinced me that I was a boy again, and that I had simply been dreaming an unusually long dream". He had not yet reached the stage in his career when he would ask "Which was the dream?", but the experience renewed his desire to complete at last *The Adventures of Huckleberry Finn*. The block had occurred at the end of Chapter 16 when the raft, on which the white boy, Huck, is trying to effect the escape of the black slave, Jim, has drifted in fog past Cairo, at the confluence of the Mississippi and the Ohio rivers, and the fugitives have abandoned it as a steamer bears down on it in the dark. Plot construction was not Mark Twain's strongest suit, and he seems not to have seen his way forward. To take an escaping slave further down the Mississippi was illogical: after Cairo he needed to head Jim north-east into free territory, but how best to do this had temporarily proved, as Huck would have said, "too many for him". Scholarly work on the manuscripts is too complex to summarize here, illuminating as it is in reconstructing his possible thought-processes, but the revisionist view of the

ante-bellum South bred in him by his trip may have suggested the concept of the uglier, more violent and reactionary region that most of the remainder of the story documents.

The earlier part of the story has been more in key with *Tom Sawyer* in the boyish scrapes the two get into, but even so this is clearly a less idyllic Hannibal: it contains slaves, who are less than content with their lot, Huck's drunken father, who is aggressively resistant to all efforts at reforming him, and Huck, a social outcast whose questioning of accepted morality, amusing as it is in its naïveté, indicates a non-conformity absent from the earlier book. His determination to run away, and especially his decision to take Jim with him, indicates a potential maturity quite beyond Tom. For the first sixteen chapters the withdrawal of the boy and the black from the town to the river consolidates their friendship in conversations, in which both are equally unsophisticated, and in the simple enjoyment of drifting on a raft through the tranquillity of a beautiful, natural riverscape. Only the occasional necessity of going ashore for provisions renews contact with a world that is less congenial, though not yet hostile. Once Cairo is past, Mark Twain seems to

HUCKLEBERRY FINN *(left),* "juvenile pariah", *first appeared in* Tom Sawyer *where he was dreaded by the village mothers and admired by their children. Dressed in the cast-off clothes of full-grown men, his* "hat was a vast ruin with a wide crescent lopped out of its brim . . . but one suspender supported his trousers".

FILM POSTER *(above) for the 1974 Universal version of* Huckleberry Finn, *directed by J. Lee Thompson.*

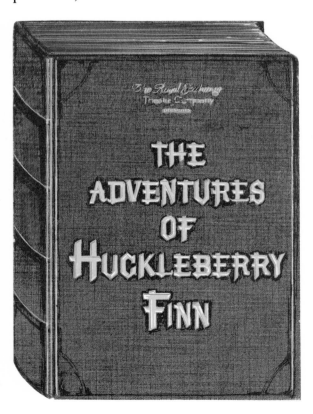

THEATRE PROGRAMME *(left) for* The Adventures of Huckleberry Finn, *a play based on Twain's novel, written and directed by David Terence and first performed at the Royal Exchange Theatre, Manchester on 19 May 1977.*

HUCK FINDS A RUNAWAY
(above). "It was Miss Watson's
Jim! I bet I was glad to see him. I
says: 'Hello, Jim!' and skipped
out. He bounced up and stared at
me wild. Then he drops down on
his knees and puts his hand
together and says: 'Doan' hurt me
– don't! I hain't ever done no
harm to a ghos'.'"

ifestation of what Mark Twain had cen-
sured in the previous book as "the jejune
romanticism of an absurd past that is
dead"). Emmeline herself, Huck learns,
went into a decline when she could not find
a rhyme for the name of one dead person –
Whistler. "She warn't ever the same after
that; she never complained" (another echo
of Judge Oliver), "but she kinder pined
away and did not live long". Like Jim
Smiley's dog, whose demise is similarly described in "The Jumping Frog", she accepts
that the world has no place for the failed
professional: the recurrence of all these
themes, even in so grotesque a context, is
inescapable. Shortly afterwards, Huck encounters death first-hand, and in sterner
form, when the feud is suddenly refuelled
by the elopement of Sophia Grangerford
and Harney Shepherdson: the ensuing
gunfights leave dead, among others, Huck's
new-found friend, Buck Grangerford, a
boy of his own age. Mark Twain's scepticism
about the damage romantic love can do has
persisted since *The Innocents Abroad*.

Huck rejoins Jim, who has rediscovered
the raft, but their hopes that they are now
"free and safe once more" are quickly
dashed when, credulously, they welcome
aboard the raft two confidence tricksters
who claim to be the rightful King of France
and a duke. There is an unpleasant side to
the otherwise amusing chicanery by which
these two raise money at a camp meeting,
and to the theatrical entertainment they
plan as their next money-spinner, although
the pseudo-Shakespearean speech they
concoct out of fragments misremembered
from *Hamlet* and *Macbeth* is hilarious.

Before the show can be put on in a little
Arkansas riverside town Huck witnesses
another murder there, this time of a drunk-
en challenger shot down in the street by one
Colonel Sherburn. This piece of Southern
chivalry threatens to end in a lynching, but
that is averted by Sherburn's self-control in
standing his ground (admittedly holding a
shotgun) and lashing the crowd with his
tongue into retreating as the cowards he
tells them they are. Tacitly the incident
creates two problems for the reader: is
Sherburn to be condemned as a haughty,
cold-blooded assassin, or admired for rout-
ing the crowd by the self-controlled calm-
ness of manner that has always drawn a

realize that neither the raft nor the plot can
drift any longer in this way.

Huck's next visit ashore involves him at
once in the unpleasant reality of a feud – a
distorted by-product of the Southern code
of chivalry – between the Grangerford
family and the Shepherdsons. The
Grangerfords take him in, and he makes
the acquaintance of death, first vicariously
in the sentimentally lugubrious poems of
Emmeline Grangerford (implicitly a man-

stunned tribute from Clemens? And how deep is Clemens's democratic faith in the people, if he presents them *en masse* so unfavourably? He gives us no more guidance than Huck, whose reaction is typical: "I could 'a' stayed if I wanted to, but I didn't want to", and so the boy slips under the canvas into a circus tent instead. He is still gullible enough, in spite of all his experiences, to be taken in when the ring is "invaded" by a performer pretending to be a drunken stranger.

The show put on by the king and the duke is so blatant a fraud, however, that having taken the money, they, Huck and Jim are obliged to leave town very rapidly. Huck is still immature enough to see only the funny side of it, but their confidence trick at the next stop, when they pose as long-lost English relatives of a newly bereaved family, with a view to putting up to auction their property, including their slaves, so outrages the boy that he exposes their duplicity. The spectacle of their being consequently tarred, feathered and "ridden out of town on a rail", though, prompts in him only pity for "them poor pitiful rascals" and the realization that "Human beings *can* be awful cruel to one another".

A TYPICAL RIVER STEAMER (above) created for the 1974 film Huckleberry Finn (Universal).

Huck is learning fast, for by now he has also gone through the moral crisis that is one of the book's distinctions. His decision to rescue Jim has always been attended by the fear that he will be thought "a low-down Abolitionist". Like his author at his age, he "was not aware that there was anything wrong about" slavery, and he constantly returns to the unpleasant knowledge that freeing Jim, who is Miss Watson's property, is theft. Reluctantly determined to do the right thing, he composes a letter telling her where she can recover her runaway, but the memory of Jim's loyalty and friendship throughout all their adversity makes him tear it up, with the deceptively simple decision, " 'All right then, I'll *go* to hell!' " It is this, in conjunction with his response to the fate of the two rogues, that prompts his strictures on the uselessness of conscience (quoted above in Chapter 1), reiterated throughout the book.

At this point Mark Twain seems to realize that the freeing of Jim has been overlooked in his concentration on violence, villainy, fraud and gullibility in a South strangely unlike that of *Tom Sawyer*, and he moves to what is, by general consent, an unusually disappointing strategy for resolving the plot. Huck and Jim have taken refuge with the Phelpses, not knowing that Tom Sawyer is their nephew and is expected on a visit. Huck is, in fact, mistaken for Tom and does not disillusion them, but when the real Tom arrives, to Huck's surprise and relief, he not only protects Huck by pretending to be his

HUCK'S DRUNKEN FATHER HALLUCINATES (left). "I don't know how long I was asleep, but all of a sudden there was an awful scream and I was up. There was pap, looking wild and skipping around every which way and yelling about snakes. He said they was crawling up his legs: and then he would give a jump and scream, and say one had bit him on the cheek – but I couldn't see no snakes" (Huckleberry Finn).

JIM THE RUNAWAY SLAVE
(right), as portrayed by Paul
Winfield in the 1974 film
Huckleberry Finn (Universal).

HUCK CANOES AFTER THE RAFT
(opposite left). "When I got to it
Jim was setting there with his
head down between his knees,
asleep, with his right arm hangin
over the steering oar"
(Huckleberry Finn).

THE HUCKLEBERRY FINN HOUSE
(below) in Hannibal, Missouri,
was a short walk from the
Clemens' house. Tom
Blankenship, model for
Huckleberry Finn, lived there.
The house has now been
demolished.

own brother Sid, but offers to help accomplish Jim's release. Huck's anti-Abolitionist conscience tells him he should prevent Tom from bringing his family into disrepute by stealing a slave, but inertia leads him to go along with yet another of Tom's wild schemes, only to discover, when the plan has nearly brought them all to grief, that Tom has known all the time that Miss Watson, dying, had set Jim free in her will before Tom's arrival at the Phelpses.

The ending is unsatisfactory for three reasons. Bringing Tom back into the story alters its entire tone, the grotesque role into which Tom's scheme forces Huck and Jim degrades unacceptably the stature of the two as characters, and the whole moral thrust of the book is threatened. The second of these is especially prejudicial to the presentation of Jim. The patient loyalty and friendship with which he has, throughout the journey, accepted Huck's congenital attitude of racial superiority and tolerated the thoughtless tricks into which it has led the boy, Jim's attitude towards his own family, his dignified courage in the face of adversity – all these make Mark Twain's portrayal of him a landmark in nineteenth-century American presentation of a black character.

Present-day complaints against the use of the term "nigger" throughout ignore the reality of historical fact: the term was in common use, and among both races. Far more significant than the mere word, in the context of the 1880s, is the powerful irony in the passage at the end of Chapter 15, when Jim's goodness elicits an apology even from Huck: "It was fifteen minutes before I could work myself up to go and humble myself to a nigger, but I done it, and I warn't ever sorry for it afterward, neither."

Accusations of a patronizing attitude behind the rendering of the black dialect and of some of the more superstitious, credulous and unsophisticated aspects of character similarly underestimate the affectionate, even respectful, care Mark Twain gave to the writing of it. In *Life on the Mississippi* he had praised Joel Chandler Harris as "the only master the country has produced" in reproducing that dialect, but his own attempts were creditable and sincerely meant. Yet it cannot be denied that his attitude to the blacks, however enlightened by the standards of his day, is not helped by his failure to see the damage he does it in this final grotesque section of the novel.

To the extent that *Huckleberry Finn* is a novel of initiation, unlike the more static *Tom Sawyer*, the intention, if not the detailed execution, of the final part can be defended. The central irony of the fable is that Huck is always convinced that what he is doing instinctively is wrong by the conventional moral code of the day, but he still does it. Mark Twain himself was to speak of it as a novel about "a sound heart and a deformed conscience". In any crisis Huck's reactions are first, to wish he was dead; second, to wish Tom Sawyer was there to tell him what to do; third, to do what comes naturally to him, and thereby save the day. Wisely, Mark Twain does not attribute to Huck the power of articulating what he has learnt from his experiences along the river, but the reader surely looks for some realization on the boy's part that Tom is in no sense his superior. That is what the final episodes, albeit clumsily, may be seen to imply. Huck's final decision to "light out for the territory ahead of the rest" in his continued resistance to the Phelpses' new attempt to "sivilize" him is indicative of wish-fulfilment on the part of his author, and foreshadows the disillusion with civilization that becomes more prominent in Mark Twain's later works.

"All modern American literature", said Ernest Hemingway in a much-quoted generalization, "comes from one book by Mark Twain called *Huckleberry Finn*. . . . It's the best book we've had." The tribute is not undeserved. More than any other single work, it established what has become known as "the Vernacular Tradition" as the appropriate mode for American literature. All major nineteenth-century American writers had accepted Emerson's dictum, "We have listened too long to the courtly muses of Europe". It took the Southern idiom of a fictitious young illiterate to silence those muses, and a Western humorist to legitimize a non-literary language as an effective counterblast to "the Sir Walter disease". Mark Twain may not have realized the full significance of his achievement, however: characteristically disappointed with sales, in a letter to his London pub-

lisher he attributed the poor results in England exclusively to "that unchristian dialect" which non-Americans could not be expected to understand.

Even in the United States it did not sell when it first appeared in 1885. It was attacked by many newspapers and critics for its coarseness and violence, though Joel Chandler Harris stood up for it. Only its banning from the public library in Concord, Massachusetts, tipped the scales: when that was known, sales began to soar. This was especially gratifying to Clemens, because, disillusioned with Osgood, he had set up his own publishing house, run by his nephew, as Charles L. Webster and Company. Inevitably this had strained his resources, but then one illustration in the first printing was found to depict Silas Phelps apparently indecently exposing himself, and the printing had to be withdrawn at further expense. An unsuccessful lawsuit to prevent a New York bookseller from selling it at a cut rate also proved costly, so that Clemens was once more in financial straits.

The theatre did not want his dramatizations of *Tom Sawyer*, *The Prince and the Pauper* or the Colonel Sellers play he and Howells had written, and he needed more money still to invest in the Paige typesetting machine. Accordingly, he returned to the lecture-circuit, this time touring with George Washington Cable, giving readings from their works, and then, hearing that General Grant was writing his *Personal Memoirs*, Clemens foresaw a major publishing coup and secured the rights for his company. Before looking at his business fortunes further, however, it will be more convenient once again to ignore chronology and refer to the only other of his major works to deal with the South.

The Tragedy of Pudd'nhead Wilson, to use its full title, appeared in 1894, but has attracted particular attention in recent years, when events have given it a new topicality. Set in 1830 in Dawson's Landing, a small town on the Mississippi, it traces the development of two boys, born on the same day in the same house, one to its patrician owner, the other to his slave, Roxana. The two children are indistinguishable in their whiteness, Roxana's not merely because his unidentified father was white, but because she is herself only one-sixteenth black. Thus her son, Chambers, is only one-thirty-second black, but this is sufficient for him to be classified as black and, of course, a slave. The significance of this is quietly emphasized by Mark Twain's description of the master as "a fairly humane man towards slaves and other animals". Fearful of the possibility of her son being sold down the river, Roxana takes advantage of his colour to switch him in the cradle with Tom, the child of the house, convinced that she has given her offspring a better start in life.

It becomes quickly apparent that Chambers (now Tom) is an unlikeable, fractious child, quick-tempered, domineering and devious, as the two boys grow up into their teens. At the death of her master, Roxana is

set free, but as this only means that she now has nowhere to live, she leaves to become a chambermaid on a riverboat, while Tom (now Chambers), of course, remains in slavery. The new Tom spends a short time at Yale and a lot of money at gambling and similar activities, but his debts are paid for him by his trusting "uncle", Judge Driscoll. Nevertheless, when Roxana, forced out of employment by rheumatism, seeks support from Tom, he spurns her and she tells him his true identity. To pay off more debts he resorts to thefts, but the exasperated Roxana tries her best to control him, while forcing him to support her financially.

Matters come to a dramatic pitch when Tom insults one of a pair of Italian twins, who have settled in Dawson's Landing, is assaulted by him, and takes him to court. This outrages his "uncle" who, as a Southern gentleman from one of the first families of Virginia, disowns him for not having challenged Luigi to a duel instead of suing him. Tom's continued refusal to challenge the Italian forces the judge to do so himself, and honour is satisfied when they meet. Anxiety about the continued thefts and housebreaking is later increased when the judge is found murdered, and it is at this point that Pudd'nhead Wilson, whose role

has been relatively passive, comes into his own as the title leads us to expect.

Wilson is an eccentric who, despite his legal training, has never had a case to handle. He lives by casual employment as an accountant, with ample time to pursue the hobbies that have served to earn him his nickname. Prominent among these are palmistry, the new science of fingerprints, the devising of sardonic aphorisms to ornament

HUCK AND TOM SAWYER DIG THEIR WAY THROUGH TO JIM *(far left).* "*So we dug and dug, with the case-knives, till most midnight; and then we was dog-tired, and our hands was blistered, and yet you couldn't see we'd done anything, hardly*" (Huckleberry Finn).

HUCK AND JIM BY THE RIVER *(above right) in a scene from the 1974 film* Huckleberry Finn.

HUCK AND JIM SEE A WRECKED STEAMBOAT *(left).* "*The lightning showed her very distinct. She was leaning over, with part of her upper deck above water, and you could see every little chimbly-guy clean and clear*" (Huckleberry Finn).

SAMUEL CLEMENS' LIBRARY *at the Hartford House in Connecticut, photographed by R. S. de Lamater, 1885.* Harper's New Monthly Magazine *reported in October 1885: "The library which appears to be the favourite of the household reveals at one end an exquisite glimpse of a little winding stream . . ."*

MARK TWAIN'S HANDPRINT *(opposite, bottom), made by the palmist Count Louis Hamon, better known as "Cheiro".*

incontrovertibly from his large collection of fingerprints; these represent most of the inhabitants of Dawson's Landing and have been taken at various points in their lives. He even happens to have fingerprinted the two infant changelings before Roxana had devised her plan. Interpreting in full the complex message of the fingerprints and seeing through Tom's disguise is then a matter of rational deduction.

Outlined thus, the novel may seem little more than an entertaining period piece that relies on the topicality of identification by fingerprint, and strains the improbability of coincidence relatively little more than dozens of others. Although shorter and more tightly plotted than his other novels, it still leaves an extravagant number of loose ends which function less as the deliberate red herrings in the conventional detective story than as distractions. An explanation is appended, in a characteristically teasing "Author's Note", to the effect that it began as two discrete stories, between which the author only belatedly saw a relationship; reluctant to remove, in the process of merging them, any of the characters he had created, he retained them even when they were no longer essential. Indifference to detail and to artistic unity is not unprecedented in Mark Twain when he has grown tired of working on a book, and some readers may be less troubled than others by his failure to develop the young Rowena into the female lead she seems intended to be, or by the lack of any reason why the symmetry between two interchangeable children and a pair of identical Italian twins is introduced but unexploited. (This latter point is inadequately explained merely by one of the two original stories having been about a pair of Siamese twins.)

More interesting questions relate to the book's inner theme. After a short but delightful opening chapter, its Southern setting is not employed for local colour, regional atmosphere or nostalgia to the extent that it has been in his earlier books; indeed, rather more of it would not have been unwelcome. The pride of Judge Driscoll and others of his class in their "first families of Virginia" ancestry is viewed indulgently rather than mocked, and their adherence to the code of chivalry that requires gentlemen to fight duels is unquestioned, *Life on*

a calendar, and serving as sole member of the Freethinkers' Society of which Judge Driscoll is President. Held in contempt by the general populace, he is nevertheless regarded with respect and some awe by the main characters in the novel, despite losing his first case when he defends Luigi.

The intricacies of the plot need not be followed in further detail here. Its logic clearly requires an ending in which Wilson will penetrate Tom's disguise as a woman, reveal that the burglaries were committed by him, that he is the judge's murderer, and is in reality no Driscoll but Roxana's son. All but the first of these Wilson can establish

the Mississippi notwithstanding. Historically accurate to the 1830s it may be, but that is not usually a prime consideration for Mark Twain. Similarly, the smallness of the community makes more credible the possibility of Wilson's fingerprinting most members more than once in their lives, but Dawson's Landing is immediately and precisely located on the Mississippi. As in *Huckleberry Finn*, the backwardness, prejudice and reactionary predilections of the inhabitants of such towns are an integral element of the novel, but these qualities are by no means unique to the Old South.

What dictates place, period and plot is one issue: slavery. Mark Twain's willingness to strain credulity by his insistence on the whiteness of Roxana and her son underlines this. Twentieth-century liberalism will be more shocked than Clemens's contemporaries at so rigorous a classification of colour, but even in 1894 it must have aroused some uneasiness. Yet, in *Pudd'n-head Wilson* even this is a means to another end rather than a primary target. That end is the dramatization, in fictional form, of a theory of environmental determinism

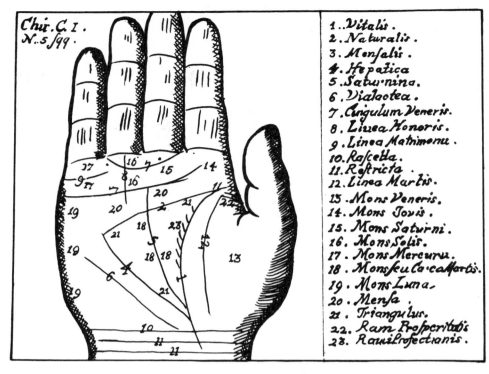

A SEVENTEENTH-CENTURY NOMENCLATURE OF THE PALM *(above). One of Pudd'nhead's pet fads is palmistry, and his habit of fingerprinting the local people helps to identify a murderer.*

which had been popular at the time. An interest in this had been evident in Mark Twain's earlier works still to be discussed here, but in this novel it is most starkly presented. One of Pudd'nhead Wilson's maxims is: "Training is everything. The peach was once a bitter almond: cauliflower is nothing but cabbage with a college education." In a country holding, as a self-evident truth, "that all men are created equal", the factors that so patently differentiate them must be sought elsewhere than in their birth: where better than in the custom of the country that makes some free and some slaves? Even in 1894 slavery was still an issue too sensitive for wholly uninhibited discussion, and it was one on which Samuel Clemens's own views had undergone considerable change; his courage in tackling it at all deserves respect.

Fear of miscegenation and its implications had not been abolished with slavery, and to reduce to one thirty-second part the distinguishing element is a challenge, not a concession, to notions of white supremacy. It makes more credible the possibility of the interchange required by the plot; it might also be thought (and not merely by Roxana) that the slave is being given the best possible head-start. If he still comes to grief (and even after a college education), it is not his heredity that has betrayed him, but the failure of those who, in his early training,

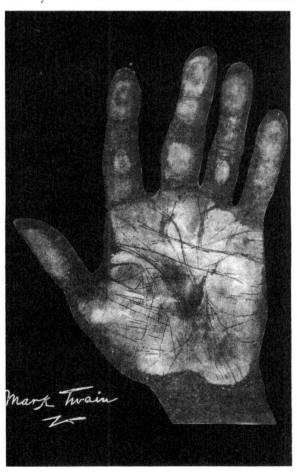

PUDD'NHEAD WILSON (below): having electrified the court by identifying the fingerprints of Count Luigi and Count Angelo, Puddn'head asks "Am I right?"

SUGAR CANE PLANTATION *(right). Although slavery had been legally abolished by the time* Tom Sawyer, Huckleberry Finn *and* Pudd'nhead Wilson *were written, Twain set all three novels in the slaveholding society of the Southern states in which he had grown up.*

have pampered him excessively. Perhaps evasively, the "white" Tom, translated to slavery, receives less attention in the story, but a paragraph in the final chapter poignantly epitomizes him as the worse case: restored to his "rightful" status, but utterly and irredeemably unfitted for it by the illiteracy and lack of the social training imposed on him by his upbringing in the slave quarters. Yet, being "free", he is automatically debarred from returning to where he was at least at ease.

It is a demonstrably oversimplified thesis and in some respects even confused, especially in what, for the purpose of the fable, it leaves unquestioned. If training is everything, why does the sense of white superiority inculcated into the false "Tom" not extend to the code of chivalry so admired by his uncle? If a slave environment is so totally destructive, how is it that Roxana, who approaches her son in his new role as master "with all the wheedling and supplicating servilities that fear and interest can impart to the words and attitudes of the born slave", is capable of the love and self-sacrifice that enable her to suggest he sells her back into slavery, or of the strength of mind and purpose to try to help him out of the morass of his own turpitude? Or whence did Jim, in *Huckleberry Finn*, derive his nobility of character?

It is not required of a novelist that his collected works display a coherent philosophy, but if it were, Mark Twain provides an answer in a casual comment of Pudd'nhead's: "It ain't a philosophy at all – it's a fact. And there is something pathetic and beautiful about it, too." It is also a fact about which there is something distinctly disturbing, even today, as there is about the book's full title: *The Tragedy of Pudd'nhead Wilson*. It is a tragedy because the man it names, whose intelligence, common sense, humanity and dedication resolve, as far as they can be resolved, the tragedies of others, has spent most of the book – and his life – on the sidelines. Worse, he has been actively despised as a fool by those who are unable to recognize his virtues and utterly fail to appreciate the trenchant truths behind the mordant wit of the maxims in his Calendar that introduce every chapter. Like the true Tom's, his vindication comes too late to compensate for the waste of his earlier life in a hostile environment. Mark Twain is beginning to see this as his own – and the human – condition.

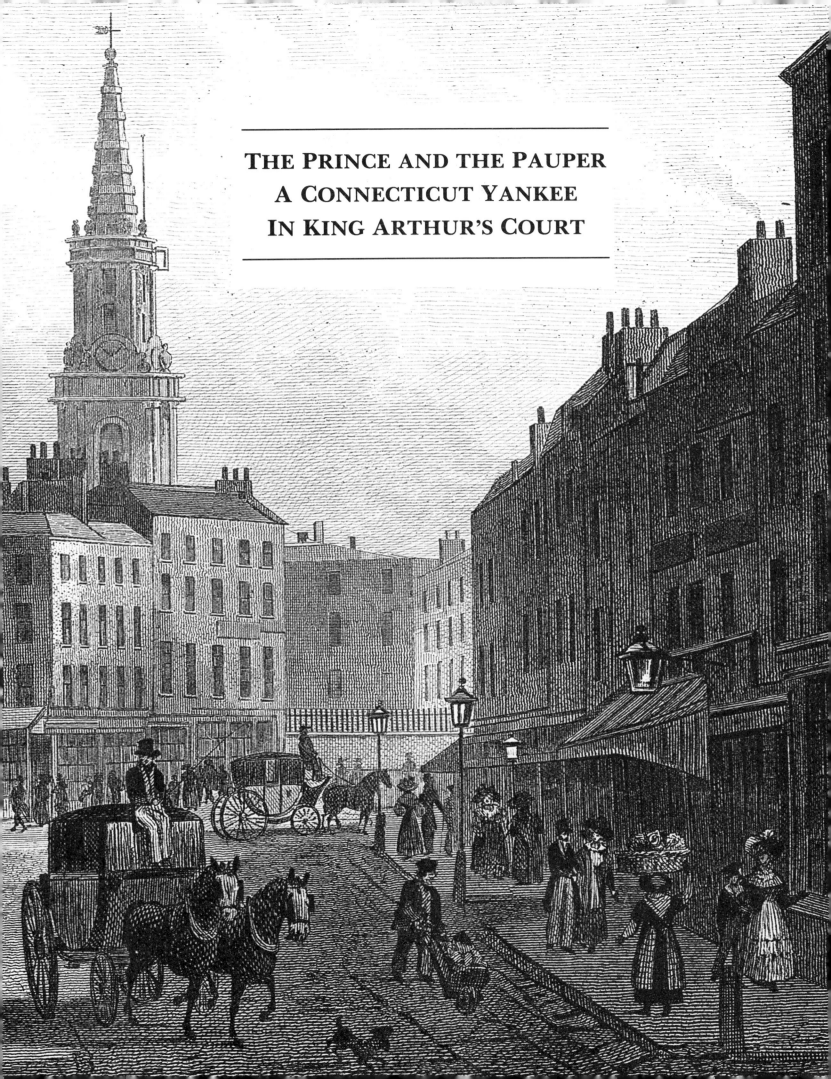

THE PRINCE AND THE PAUPER
A CONNECTICUT YANKEE
IN KING ARTHUR'S COURT

THE BRITISH ISLES

LONDON.

DUBLIN.

SCALE

EDINBURGH

SHETLAND ISLANDS

ORKNEY ISLANDS

IRISH SEA

ST GEORGES CHANNEL

CARDIGAN BAY

BRISTOL CHANNEL

ENGLISH CHANNEL

CHANNEL ISLANDS

FRANCE

Meridian of Greenwich.

MARK TWAIN AND BRITAIN

Having been born only fifty-nine years after the United States had formally declared its independence from Great Britain, Samuel L. Clemens was as ambivalent in his attitude to the former mother country as most of his contemporaries. Like many of them, he was not above clinging to any genealogical evidence, however tenuous, of a possible British origin. Later in his life he went to considerable trouble to secure a facsimile of the death warrant for King Charles I, proudly claiming descent from one of its signatories, Gregory Clemens. Moreover, a distant relative of his mother's family, the Lamptons, Jesse M. Leathers of Kentucky, was convinced that he was the rightful heir to the Earl of Durham. Sam affected an amused scepticism about this, but, though it clashed with his democratic principles, he was fascinated by the possibility.

By the 1870s there was a rapidly rising tide of Americans trying to establish such claims to English estates by any possible means, and even by some wildly unrealistic ones. In London in 1873 the popular press was following avidly the affair of the Tichborne Claimant, and, being in England at the time, so was Mark Twain, even though no American interests were involved. He not only had his secretary fill six large scrap-books with newspaper clippings, but himself spent an evening in the company of the central figure, "Sir Roger Tichborne", the long-missing heir to the family estate. Although Clemens seems to have been impressed by him, the court was not, and Arthur Orton, the man in question, served

a fourteen-year prison term for the impersonation. This theme of identity, falsely claimed or mistaken, will be seen to become increasingly important in his later work (Huck Finn being taken for Tom Sawyer, the activities of the "King" and the "Duke", and the central situation of *Pudd'nhead Wilson* have already been encountered). Initially, however, Mark Twain's primary interest in England had been more directly mercenary – as a market for his books.

His earliest experiences in this had encouraged Anglophobia: in the absence of any law of International Copyright, the

LONDON FOG (*above*). *When lecturing to an English audience on a particularly foggy evening, Twain remarked, "Perhaps you can't see me, but I am here."*

THE TRIAL OF CHARLES I,, *1649 (left). Twain claimed to be descended from a seventeenth-century Clemens who was a member of the court that sentenced Charles I to death.*

NINETEENTH-CENTURY MAP OF BRITAIN (*opposite*) *by John Tallis. Always eager to extend their knowledge of Britain, Twain and his family travelled as extensively as possible on their many visits, exploring Sussex, Warwickshire, Shropshire, Lancashire, the Lake District, Edinburgh and elsewhere, as well as living for a year in London.*

"Jumping Frog" and other pieces had been
unscrupulously pirated, and works not by
his hand had been foisted upon him. Fore-
most in this activity had been the London
publisher, John Camden Hotten, too complex a character to merit the customary
dismissal of him as a mere pirate and por-
nographer. He was both, but he was also
something of a scholar and, as in his pub-

lishing of Swinburne, a champion of the
avant-garde, as well as a shrewd business-
man. Becoming familiar at first-hand,
through visiting the States, with the new
humorous writing of the American West,
Hotten recognized a commodity for which
an English taste could be developed.

Piracy was, of course, as Dickens and
other British writers had already found out
to their cost, just as rife and perhaps even
more lucrative in American publishing
practice. Ignoring that, Mark Twain was
prompt in realizing the publicity value of a
display of righteous indignation. Consequently, on his first visit to England in 1872,
he published in the *Spectator* a vigorous
attack on "John Camden Hottentot" (as he
renamed him) and his methods. By now,
though, *Roughing It* had reached a British
market on the more reputable lists of
George Routledge & Sons, and one of the
reasons for Clemens's visit was to develop a
personal contact with the Routledges and to
discuss an authorized English edition of *The
Innocents Abroad*. (Hotten had pirated it in
1871.) Although Clemens found the Routledge family somewhat snobbish in their
formality, at least they paid him copyright
on his books, the "moral grandeur" of
which he acknowledged in a Preface specially drafted for the forthcoming edition.

On reflection, he decided that the draft
as a whole was "not at all in good taste" and
not suited to "so reserved and dignified a
people as the English", and substituted one
rather more ingratiating, claiming to have
revised the text of the whole book lest he
offend them. Yet before leaving America
he had ideas of writing a "telling book about
the English", probably on the lines of *The
Innocents Abroad*. His English reputation
and the warmth of his reception so took
him by surprise that this idea seems quickly

to have evaporated when he found, as he observed in his notebook, "the English singularly cordial in their welcome and hearty in their hospitality".

The Routledges took him to the Savage Club, and, with the poet Tom Hood, to Brighton. At a concert at the Albert Hall the Sheriff of London invited him to the Sheriff's dinner, to the ceremony of electing the Lord Mayor, and, more instructively than convivially, to see a trial at the Old Bailey. He visited Regent's Park and the Zoo, was given a privately conducted tour of the British Museum and was allowed to use the Reading Room undisturbed. In

THE ALBERT HALL, KENSINGTON (*far left*). *While attending a concert here Twain was invited by the Sheriff of London to the Sheriff's dinner, to an Old Bailey trial, and to the ceremony of electing the Lord Mayor.*

HENRY VII'S CHAPEL, WESTMINSTER ABBEY (*left*), *the last addition to the abbey, was completed in 1519. Twain set one of the important chapters of* The Prince and the Pauper *in Westminster Abbey.*

THE BRITISH MUSEUM, BLOOMSBURY (*below*), *engraving by Thomas Shepherd c. 1850. By Twain's time this facade had been replaced by the more imposing classical one we know today, and the Reading-Room he visited was the present-day one.*

THE ALBERT MEMORIAL, KENSINGTON (right), designed by Gilbert Scott R.A., was opened in 1872, although the fourteen-foot high statue was not added until 1876. The monument was described by Twain as "the most genuinely humorous idea I have met with in this grave land".

DICKENS' GRAVE IN POETS' CORNER (right), part of the south transept of Westminster Abbey. Twain was pleased to see that flowers were still being placed here two years after the writer's death.

Westminster Abbey he was delighted to find people still placing flowers on the grave of Dickens, who had died two years earlier. Less reverently, he admired the Albert Memorial as "The finest monument in the world erected to glorify – the *Commonplace*. It is the most genuinely humorous idea I have met with in this grave land."

He also met a celebrity whose reception in London was very different from his own and whose reputation in America was much higher than in Britain. This was Arthur M. Stanley, the explorer who had discovered Dr Livingstone in Africa in 1871. Not only was that claim to fame being challenged at the time (though it was vindicated later), but so was Stanley's nationality. Thought of as an American, having fought in the Civil War and become well-known as a journalist there, Stanley was in fact the illegitimate son of a Welshman, John Rowlands, and had shipped from Liverpool as a cabin-boy in 1858. In New Orleans he had been adopted by Henry Morton Stanley, a merchant, who allowed him to take the same

STANLEY THE EXPLORER *(1841–1904) (below), though Welsh by birth, had been adopted by an American and served in the Confederate Army. In 1872 he returned to London after reached Livingstone in Africa, only to find that his account of the event was not believed.*

name. Mark Twain had had an earlier in-direct encounter with Stanley when the latter, reporting a lecture Clemens gave in 1867 in his home state of Missouri, re-printed so much of the text as to destroy any possibility of its author repeating the lecture elsewhere. Stanley's situation in London in 1872 as a discredited claimant, with a story that seemed stranger than fiction, must have added fuel to Mark Twain's interest in such matters, and their paths were to cross again later.

In view of his own popularity in Britain it is small wonder that he returned in the spring of 1873 accompanied by his wife, their daughter Susy, and a Miss Clara Spaulding as nurse to Susy and companion to Olivia. Again their range of friends increased quickly. Two may be mentioned in particular. When Olivia needed medical attention in Edinburgh one name came immediately to her husband's mind, that of Dr John Brown. To the Clemenses, as to thousands across the world, the Edinburgh doctor was already loved and famous as the author of many delightful essays with a predominantly Scottish flavour, published from 1858 onwards. So, on an August morning, in 1873, it was to Dr John Brown that he turned successfully for professional advice on Olivia's indisposition.

DR. JOHN BROWN (*seated*), *with Twain, Olivia and Clara Spaulding holding Susy. Taken in August 1873 when Twain and his party first met the Edinburgh physician and author with whose delightful essays they had long been familiar. They maintained the friendship by correspondence until Dr Brown died nine years later.*

SIR WALTER SCOTT (*1771– 1832*) (*right*), *romantic novelist and poet, had provoked Twain's condemnation in* Life on the Mississippi. *Scott is here painted with some of his best-known creations by E. F. Skinner.*

They regularly accompanied him on his rounds, relaxing in his carriage with books and grapes while he paid his visits. Clemens relished Brown's exhortation to "Entertain yourselves while I go in here and reduce the population!", and they all posed for a studio photograph together. The party paid the routine visit to Sir Walter Scott's home at Abbotsford, and Brown may have helped Mark Twain in the assiduous ten-day search for the rare twelve-volume Abbotsford Edition of Scott's works. His determination to acquire this counterpoints neatly his well-known strictures on Scott in *Life on the Mississippi*. It was in New Orleans, at the end of his journey down that river with Cable in 1882, that Clemens read of the death of Dr Brown, "that noble and beautiful soul" as he described him.

In the intervening nine years the friendship had flourished in correspondence, and indeed it was in a letter to Brown with a copy of *The Gilded Age* that Mark Twain definitively identified the thirty-two chapters of the book that he himself had written. Two of John Brown's essays would have appealed to him particularly. One was the celebrated "Rab and his Friends", with its emphasis on the relationship between dogs and humans. The other was on Mar-

jorie Fleming, the precocious little girl who was reputed to have been the friend of Sir Walter Scott and had died at the age of eight. The Victorians would have been less amazed than modern readers at her creative ability and her preternatural knowledge of and love for literature, and less equivocal in their response to her piety, theological knowledge and wisdom. Nevertheless, Brown's account so engagingly establishes her more childlike attributes and describes the games she and Scott played together that Clemens at once identified her with Susy, who, at the age of fourteen months, was developing her own version of such a friendship with the widowed, sexagenarian doctor, to his great delight. One of the last pieces Mark Twain was to publish, in 1909, the year before his death, was a re-telling of Marjorie's story in *Harper's Bazaar* as "The Wonder Child". By that time, in his loneliness, the identification with his now-dead daughter was complete.

It was on this visit also that Clemens made the acquaintance of an expatriate Southerner living in London, Moncure Daniel Conway. Three years older than Clemens, Conway came from a Virginian slave-

ABBOTSFORD HOUSE (*left*) on the banks of the River Tweed in Roxburgh, was home of Sir Walter Scott, who transformed it from a modest farmhouse into a Gothic-style baronial mansion. Twain visited Abbotsford with Dr. Brown.

owning family, but, abandoning their Methodism for Unitarianism, he had been converted also to the Abolitionist cause and was sent to London in 1863 to gain British support. Less than wholly successful in this errand, he had stayed on to become the Minister of the South Place Ethical Society, a humanist community still extant in London and now housed in a hall in Red Lion Square named after him. Conway also supported himself and his family by lecturing and by freelance journalism. Making himself known to many leading British and American writers of the day, he also came to function as an unofficial, self-appointed, but very effective cultural liaison officer.

Quickly contacting the latest famous American writer to arrive in London, Conway helped the Clemenses to acclimatize themselves and took them on outings. For them the most outstanding of these was the visit to Stratford-upon-Avon. Here Conway had arranged for them to be received and entertained by the Mayor, Mr Charles Flowers, who was raising funds to establish the Shakespeare Memorial there the following year. After the usual round of sightseeing, it was from Mr Flowers that Mark Twain appreciatively "learned all about how ale is made" and acquired a "new and ferocious interest in consuming it". (Flowers are still

the Stratford brewers.)

After short and less eventful visits to Ireland and Paris, Clemens took his party back to America in October 1873 and, after a week, returned to London for the third time in twelve months. This time he was

MONCURE DANIEL CONWAY (1832–1907) (*left*), clergyman and author, was Minister of the South Place Ethical Society in Finsbury, London, from 1863 to 1884. He arranged many interesting outings in England for Twain and Olivia and later went to stay with them in Hartford.

99

SHAKESPEARE'S TOMB AND MEMORIAL (right) in Holy Trinity Church, Stratford-upon-Avon. Fund-raising for the memorial was still in progress when Twain visited the town.

ST PATRICK'S, DUBLIN (far right). Before taking his family back to America in 1873, Twain also visited Ireland.

STRATFORD-UPON-AVON (below). Conway arranged for Twain to be received by Charles Flowers, mayor of the town, and an expert on brewing.

unaccompanied and had a heavy lecture programme to complete. Again his reception was so warm that by December he was writing to Livy that "it seems as if 3 out of every 5 I meet on the street recognize me. This in London! It seems incredible". This was in large part due to his success on the lecture platform. The dry humour with which he described his experiences in the American West and in the Sandwich Islands was something that the audiences had been led to expect from his books: his Southern drawl (especially in an age when oral media were virtually unknown), the poker-faced throw-away technique of his delivery, his informality, and his impromptus were all bonuses. Lecturing on a particularly foggy night, he was moved to reassure his hearers: "Perhaps you can't see me, but I am here." In our own time Hal Holbrook's re-creations of Mark Twain's platform manner have given theatre-goers on both sides of the Atlantic an excellent understanding of the author's popularity as a lecturer, especially with his less cosmopolitan British contemporaries.

Tennyson wrote specially to tell him how he "longed to come and hear him". Shirley Brooks, the editor of Punch, not only promoted Mark Twain's lectures actively in his columns but invited him to spend New Year's Eve at his home. All this Clemens reported enthusiastically to Livy, but one invitation she must have particularly envied. She had long admired the novels of Charles Kingsley who had now, his novel-writing days behind him, become Canon of Westminster. He offered to guide Mark Twain on a private visit to "some strange & remote spots in our great Stone Mausoleum", accompanied only by the ladies of his household who were "even more fond of your work than I".

Three months later, when Kingsley was in the States, Clemens had the pleasure of inviting him to Hartford and also introducing him to an audience in Boston with a speech that, though in better taste than his later "hideous mistake" in that city, was somewhat laboured and infelicitous. As a speaker Mark Twain seems to have had a congenital difficulty in expressing the genuine respect he felt for other celebrities. The friendship might have developed well, though, had Kingsley not died at fifty-five a year later.

To his enormous satisfaction, Mark Twain was elected to the Savage Club before this visit finished, and spent Christmas at Salisbury, which, he told Livy, reminded him of Coventry Patmore's books. His familiarity with serious Victorian poetry and prose has not, perhaps, received sufficient recognition. In January 1874 he sailed home expecting to return to England shortly, but five years were to elapse before he was able to fulfil that hope.

An important friendship that was consolidated in the second 1873 visit was that with Moncure Daniel Conway, whose enthusiasm for Clemens's lectures was expressed in letters; Conway may also have been the author of some of the unsigned reviews appearing in the press. He and Clemens enjoyed each other's company and in 1875, on a lecture tour in the United States, Conway was invited to stay at the house in Hartford.

Here Mark Twain entrusted to him the manuscript of *The Adventures of Tom Sawyer* to place with a British publisher other than Routledge. By now Hotten had died suddenly, but his publishing house in Piccadilly continued in business as Chatto & Windus, and it was to them that Conway turned at once. How successful this inspiration was may be gauged by the fact that Chatto & Windus was the only publishing house, British or American, with whom Mark Twain never broke off relations in his lifetime and which has continued to pride itself, legitimately, on being his British publishers. The detailed history of this successful partnership may be found in my *Mark Twain in England* (1978) and will be referred to again in the next chapter.

Andrew Chatto had been an employee of Hotten's and, on taking over the firm in 1873 and knowing Mark Twain to be in London, had written to introduce himself and to say diplomatically that he was "sincerely anxious to establish more cordial relations as between Author & Publisher, than have hitherto existed, between your-

self and our firm". Clemens does not seem to have responded, but he must have noted with interest the names Chatto quoted of writers willing to recommend him: "Mr [Ambrose] Bierce, Mr Tom Hood, and Mr [Charles] Stoddard" – one Briton sandwiched between two Americans, and all three known personally to Mark Twain.

Conway, whose work Hotten had (legitimately) published, also knew Chatto, so his further recommendation, as well as the terms he secured for him, readily persuaded Clemens. Chatto's quick realization of the benefit, in terms of publicity and business, of adding Mark Twain to the house's lists indicates the shrewdness and enterprise that characterize his whole career, but his personality was a warm and generous one to which many authors responded. Mark Twain was no exception, and a deal was settled.

The humorist and the publisher first met in person in 1877 when Chatto was on a visit to New York. He attended the opening night of *Ah Sin* on 31 July, and they met again the next day at the Lotos Club. Clemens's next letter to Conway alternates

ALFRED, LORD TENNYSON *(1809–1892) (below), the poet laureate, wrote to Twain that he "longed to come and hear him" lecturing.*

HAL HOLBROOK *(below), modern impersonator of Twain, whose stage performances convey something of the writer's popular lecturing style.*

between vilification of Bret Harte and praise of Chatto as "a fine man & gentleman. I like him". Conway had initiated a lifelong friendship between the two men which extended quickly to their families.

When the British edition of *Tom Sawyer* appeared (as has been seen, six months before the American version), Conway's enthusiasm for it led Charles Dudley Warner, after a visit to London, to report to its author that Conway even read it to his congregation on Sundays. Certainly Conway used his reputation as a popular lecturer to support his praise of the novel from the platform with copious quotations, a technique that he employed also in reviewing it, often anonymously, in British and American journals. Indeed, in one instance his enthusiasm proved a puzzle and embar-

rassment to Mark Twain: an unsigned review by him appeared in the *Cincinnati Commercial* months before the novel was published in America at all. However, the contract Conway negotiated for him with Chatto, and the success of the book in England, encouraged Clemens to offer Conway a commission of five per cent on the royalties from Chatto's sales. This is believed to have made Conway in effect the first literary agent in history to be paid for his services, and the friendship between the two men lasted until Conway's death in New York in 1907.

The Clemenses next came to London in July 1879, intending to stay until September. This time they made the acquaintance of, among others, Charles Darwin (when visiting Windermere), and the Pre-Raphaelite painter, John Everett Millais, at a house party near Shrewsbury. In the Lake District they had been attracted to an etching by the notorious opponent of Pre-Raphaelitism, the American, James McNeill Whistler. Chatto was promptly requested to obtain it for them (if possible, at less than the advertised price of seventeen guineas) and get it to Liverpool in two days when they would be leaving for home. Over the years Chatto cheerfully executed many such commissions for them, including reserving hotel accommodation and ensuring that there were flowers in the room for Livy on arrival.

Chatto also worked out a scheme for obtaining a form of international copyright before that was legally enforceable. It entailed Mark Twain's copyrighting a book in advance with the Librarian of Congress and Chatto's depositing a copy of the English edition at Stationers' Hall in London on the day of its publication in America. Canadian piracy could be prevented only by publication of the authorized edition in Canada on the day following and provided that Mark Twain was physically on Canadian soil at the time of publication. It was cumbersome but effective: the trip from Buffalo, New York, across to Niagara was relatively painless, but close liaison between the publishing houses on both sides of the Atlantic was essential. Mark Twain's eruptions on occasions when the arrangement broke down had almost always to be directed at the American publisher rather than at

CHARLES KINGSLEY *(1819–1875) (below). Twain was offered a guided tour of Westminster Abbey by Kingsley, novelist and clergyman, who was then a canon of the abbey.*

CHARLES DARWIN *(1809–1892) (above), naturalist and author, was introduced to Twain in the Lake District.*

Chatto. Often, though, it was the author's own carelessness that was at fault in forgetting to do something he had promised.

Nevertheless, the system became so efficacious and widespread that, until the International Copyright Law of 1891, one publisher would simply announce a forthcoming title to his transatlantic counterpart with a laconic invitation to him to "simultane". The speed of transatlantic postal communication from the 1870s onwards is often a surprise even to those who recognize that the telegraph was already in operation. There is ample evidence that if a letter from Chatto to Mark Twain in Hartford, Connecticut, required an immediate answer and Clemens was in residence when it arrived, the date of his reply was normally two weeks to the day from the date on Chatto's letter. Present-day airmail is sometimes known to take as long.

The 1879 visit to England was less happy for the Clemenses than their previous experience. En route to Germany a year earlier, they had regretted, as they sailed through the English Channel, that Britain was not their destination, but the purpose of the trip was, of course, the walking tour that was to form the basis of *A Tramp Abroad*. From Germany they had gone on to Switzerland, Italy, and finally Paris, where

Clemens was able to meet the Russian novelist Ivan Turgenev and also renew his friendship with Conway. The latter enquired what he was working on, and, although he had begun work on *A Tramp Abroad* (which will be discussed in the next chapter), Clemens replied cryptically: "Well, it's about this: A man sets out from home on a long journey to do some particular thing. But he does everything except what he set out to do." It might be his own career that he was trying to epitomize, for, successful as he was, he was undeniably frustrated and disillusioned, as well as exhausted by the pace at which he had driven himself and the multifarious activities in which he had become involved.

His feud with Bret Harte was at its height and had been further fuelled by Harte's appointment as American Consul in Krefeld against Clemens's private advice to President Hayes. Not even an invitation to meet the American Ambassador in Paris, General Noyes, brought to him by Conway, assuaged that. His letters and notebooks for the period are packed with much more than attacks on Harte, though. He was obviously in bad health and this increased his irritation. Used to being lionized in London and America, he discovered that his name did not carry the same prestige in continental

IVAN TURGENEV *(1813–1883) (above). Twain met the Russian novelist in Paris in 1879, during the course of the European tour that formed the basis of* A Tramp Abroad.

LIVERPOOL (above). When Twain reached Liverpool on his way home in 1879, Chatto had arranged for one of Whistler's etchings to be waiting there for him before he left.

into the chauvinistic belief that America is purer-minded than Europe.

There was some historical basis for this. America had been much slower to recognize any aesthetic merit in the nude in art, unless it could be claimed to be serving an allegorical purpose. The American sculptor Hiram Powers's female nude, the centre of attraction at the Great Exhibition of 1851 in London, was acceptable in America only because its title, "The Greek Slave", allowed it to be seen as symbolizing chastity in the Christian captive of the Turks. As late as 1886 the American painter Thomas Eakins lost his teaching post at the Pennsylvania Academy of Fine Art for encouraging his students, of both sexes, to work from live nude models.

Clemens showed some relief on returning to London, but even there he could no longer enjoy even the theatre. He was angered by more of the snobbery he had perceived on his first visit, English humour he found more laboured than American, English church singing he thought "the perfection of the ugly", and the weather only intensified his gloom. This does not surface in his published works. Indeed, in *Life on the Mississippi* his references to the writings of English travellers, whose views on America were not always sympathetic,

Europe. Homesickness for Hartford dimmed even his desire to return to England, though he still looked forward to that visit, but he seems to have become obsessed by the double standards of morality he detected in contemporary European society.

In *The Gilded Age* he had inveighed against this in American politics, but now it was the ambivalence of sexual morality that exercised him. Doing the round of European art galleries he becomes increasingly concerned about nudity in paintings and statuary, and their effect on the beholder. Fearing lasciviousness in all the arts, he forgets the slightly prurient innuendos in his account of the girls bathing in the Sandwich Islands, and castigates eighteenth-century English novelists like Fielding and Smollett as coarse, disgusting and corrupting. This develops into an extravagant hostility towards the "bestialities" of European life and culture totally different from his earlier views and in many ways at odds with his own personality. It is also oversimplified

TOM CANTY AND THE PRINCE OF WALES EXCHANGE CLOTHES (bottom right). "The two went and stood side by side before a great mirror, and lo, a miracle: there did not seem to have been any change made" (The Prince and the Pauper).

THE PRINCE AND THE PAUPER (bottom left): scene from the 1977 film (20th Century Fox) distributed in the U.S.A. as The Crossed Swords.

are courteous. Even the attack on Sir Walter Scott is restricted, as has been seen, to what he regards as Scott's sham medievalism, and is not widened into an attack on the Old World's preoccupation with the past.

In *The Prince and the Pauper*, published in 1881, Tudor England is similarly treated with respect, even though it is clear from the notebooks and letters that his old idea of "a telling book on England" was surfacing in his mind. Howells was encouraging him in the direction of some satirical writing on European life but Mark Twain replied with a shrewd piece of self-criticism as well as a literary comment: "a man can't write successful satire except he be in a calm judicial good humor". For himself (this in January 1879), he could not feel in a good enough humour with anything to satirize it but only "to curse it and foam at the mouth". At least one of his later books might have been better had he kept that dictum longer in mind.

In England he seems to have had no public engagements and to have written few letters. A planned trip to Edinburgh was abandoned, even though Dr John Brown was in poor health and low spirits, a condition on which Olivia had written earlier to commiserate with him. Instead, on the eve of returning home from Liverpool, Clemens sent a letter of apology: everything had gone wrong, "flying trips here and there" had had to be substituted for the planned longer visits. They had, it was to prove, missed the last opportunity of seeing Brown before his death.

We know that Clemens had at least dined with Whistler and Henry James, still fulminating against Harte even to them. James, so totally different from Mark Twain as a writer and in outlook, had just published *Daisy Miller*, unknowingly diagnosing one aspect of Clemens's dilemma in the final remark made by the expatriate Winterbourne in that novel: "I was booked to make a mistake. I have lived too long in foreign parts." Not that Clemens had made any identifiable mistake, though with his overdeveloped sense of guilt he would privately have accused himself of many. It was rather that he had lost his sense of purpose and direction and, as we have seen, was to recover it only on returning to his roots on the Mississippi in 1881. Yet even that

brought him no nearer to the calm serenity of mind which he so much desired, and had so optimistically attributed to the Europeans in *The Innocents Abroad*.

In *The Prince and the Pauper* he returns to those other dichotomies that had long haunted him: identity as the product of opposing forces, heredity and environment, nature and nurture, reality and wish-fulfilment. Again he starts from the improbable situation of two people so resembling each other as to be capable of exchanging roles without discovery. The willing

THE PRINCE AND THE PAUPER (above): scene from the 1977 International Film Productions film (20th Century Fox) with a multi-star cast, including Mark Lester, Oliver Reed, Raquel Welch, Ernest Borgnine, George C. Scott, Rex Harrison, and Charlton Heston as Henry VIII.

THE PRINCE REVEALS HIMSELF *(below): "the mock-king ran with a glad face to meet him; and fell on his knees before him"* (The Prince and the Pauper).

OLD HOUSES IN HOLBORN *(opposite bottom), and entrance to Staple Inn. Twain based his description of sixteenth-century London in* The Prince and the Pauper *on half-timbered buildings like these.*

THE PRINCE AND THE PAUPER *(below): scene from the 1977 film (20th Century Fox), with Mark Lester in the dual role of Prince and Pauper.*

implications that he would explore a decade later in *Pudd'nhead Wilson* are played down in this story of tribulation borne with fortitude and justly rewarded; conscience, loyalty and moral virtue triumphant in a world where happy endings seem inevitable, and a temporary exchange of identity, innocently begun, prove beneficial to both parties and even, indirectly, to the wider community.

Set in the England of Henry VIII, the story concerns his son, the future Edward VI, and a pauper boy, Tom Canty, born in the London slums on the same day as the prince. Throughout an unhappy, underprivileged childhood, the prerequisite of the Cinderella story, Tom acquires, from the benevolence of a priest, some education and the moral strength to withstand the cruelty of his father and his wicked grandmother, from whose frequent beatings his mother is unable to protect him. His only retreat is into a dream-world of kings, princes, court life and chivalry, about which he has read, and the outward trappings of which are apparent to him from processions and public ceremonial in London. This extends into what little time for play he can find, and his playmates indulge him in innocent games of make-believe.

Chance brings him into the royal palace and the presence of the prince, at whose suggestion the two change clothes for the novelty of the experience. Chance at once leads to the expulsion of the ragged prince from the palace; Tom's fascination with royalty equips him sufficiently to avoid immediate detection, but his conduct naturally leads to the belief spreading through the court that the "prince" is mentally disturbed. A similar belief, much less sympathetically manifested, dogs the true prince, both on the unfamiliar streets he now has to wander, and in the Canty household to which chance quickly directs him.

Their respective adventures in each other's worlds need not be detailed here. Their horizons are, of course, widened, but both learn from the experience, Tom with much mental anxiety, Edward with physical suffering as well. The death of the king enables Tom to extend the humane and wise way in which he has dealt with those unfortunates with whom his princely role has brought him in touch. The prince, meanwhile, has made the acquaintance of a

suspension of disbelief that this demands of the reader is perhaps more readily achieved here by the historic remoteness of the period of the story and the fairy-tale dimension in the telling. More than any of his others, this is a children's story, as his contemporaries quickly realized, but one not to be disdained by adults. The grimmer social

loyal and faithful soldier, Miles Hendon, who, convinced of the prince's identity, tries to help him. The task is complicated, however, by Miles's wicked brother Hugh who is trying, with some success, to rob Miles of his rightful inheritance.

Eventually, on the morning of the coronation, the changelings meet each other, their identities are established, and the rightful king is crowned. Edward is a better king for his first-hand experience of the sufferings of the people; Tom is rewarded with a position that recognizes his responsible discharge of the duties he has had to assume, and lives a long and happy life. Miles, of course, regains his heritage and the woman he loves. There is, interestingly, no parallel suggestion of any love-interest in Tom's life, any more than in that of Huckleberry Finn, or of Tom Sawyer after his initial schoolboy infatuation with Becky Thatcher.

Contemporary reviewers were puzzled by this book, often making for the first time that distinction between Mark Twain and Mr Clemens that Justin Kaplan was later so firmly to establish. This was Mr Clemens's book, emphatically not Mark Twain's, and reaction to it was – and to some extent still is

– uneasy. The difference between the racy idiomatic vernacular of his earlier novels and the (self-?) consciously archaistic elevation of this was an obvious target, the mixture of documented history and improbable romance another. That Mark Twain should aim at the genteel audience delighted his family, Howells, Conway, and "Mother" Fairbanks, who had continued to encourage him in this direction, as much as it surprised and worried his friends of the Pacific slopes like Joe Goodman.

On both sides of the Atlantic there was criticism of the *hubris* that had led Mark Twain, of all people, to attempt an English historical novel, but there were also favourable comparisons with Sir Walter Scott and other writers of romance so popular at the time. What could not, obviously, have been foreseen was that, a decade later, William Morris would turn to the pastiche-medieval prose romance as a vehicle for pleading the cause of the socially down-trodden. Morris, though, had a grasp of the idiom that could not be expected of Mark Twain, a socialism that Clemens would have hesitated to espouse, though aspects of it would have been congenial to him, and an appeal to an educated adult audience that was not the

THE PRINCE'S TROUBLES BEGIN *(above) "Then followed such a thing as England had never seen before – a sacred person of the heir to the throne rudely buffeted by plebeian hands, and set upon and torn by dogs"* (The Prince and the Pauper).

MARK TWAIN *(below). Photograph taken in a London studio after 1896.*

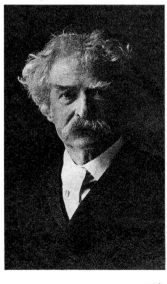

THE TRUE PRINCE INTERRUPTS
THE PAUPER'S CORONATION
*(right): "'I forbid you to set the
crown of England upon that
forfeited head. I am the king'"*
(The Prince and the Pauper).

principal target of *The Prince and the Pauper*.
Forty years earlier W. Harrison Ainsworth,
in novels like *Old St Paul's* and *The Tower of
London*, had established the historical romance for the British (as Scott had done for
the Scots); a decade later, in such novels as
The White Company and *Micah Clarke*, Arthur
Conan Doyle would mine the same vein, as
would G.A. Henty.

The first of Mark Twain's books for
which he could not draw on autobiography
and personal experience, *The Prince and the
Pauper*, gives, nevertheless, an impression
of an affectionate first-hand familiarity with
London and its past in the use it makes of
the names of streets and landmarks for
local colour. An elaborate apparatus of preface and notes documents the care with
which, over a lengthy period, Clemens had
researched the historical background to his
book, but what reviewers especially overlooked the public did not: it was essentially
a book for children, but for children of
some discrimination. Readings aloud of
work in progress to his family and friends
had provided a salutary and not uncritical
audience from whose comments he had
benefited, and what the professional critics
underestimated the public instinctively recognized, especially in Britain. Clemens was
soon able to report to an American friend
that the English sales had reached one-third
of the American, the same proportion as

THE ROYAL PALACE OF ST.
JAMES'S NEXT THE PARK *(right),
by George Cruikshank (1792–
1878). The palace was built for
Henry VIII and remained the
official residence of the soveriegn
until the time of Queen Victoria.
Twain researched the historical
background to* The Prince and
the Pauper *carefully.*

A Tramp Abroad had achieved, and the sales
of that had been regarded as very satisfac-
tory for its price. Given the difference in
size between the potential readership in the
two countries, it is a creditable result.

Chatto blithely dismissed the two hostile
reviews in *The Saturday Review* and *The
Athenaeum* because "neither of these two
papers would compliment the holy scrip-

tures, if an American had written them". An even more eloquent tribute, still preserved among the Mark Twain papers, is the letter of 1887 from nine-year-old Kate L. Corbett of Withington in Manchester. She wrote to say how much she and her brother Jack had enjoyed Tom Sawyer, Huck Finn, *Life on the Mississippi*, "but especially The Prince and the Pauper". The precocious girl even had a constructive suggestion to offer: "We have been thinking it would be a delicious History of England, if you wrote it, and made a few variations, of course, like you did in the Prince and the Pauper. It would not matter about you making it true if you made it interesting." If Mark Twain had not already been working for some time on what was to become *A Connecticut Yankee at King Arthur's Court* we might have claimed a Mancunian inspiration for that work. We do not know the reactions of the Corbett children to that book, if they read it, but they are likely to have been more tolerantly sympathetic than those of some of their elders.

George Washington Cable had introduced Clemens to Sir Thomas Malory's *Morte d'Arthur* on their trip to the South in 1882. Not for the first time Mark Twain's genuine respect for something did not prevent his attempting a well-meant burlesque of it, but the stress and problems of his private and business affairs in the 1880s darkened his mood as he worked on it fitfully between more urgent projects. Consequently it came closest to being that long-delayed "telling book on England", one of his most enigmatic, if most socially conscious works, and, for all its initial fun, one of his blackest by the end.

To see it as the product of Anglophobia, however, is to oversimplify it, for it is equally censorious of aspects of American political and commercial life and, indeed, of human nature in general. Nor should the old myth, that it had to be toned down for British publication and was unpopular in that country, be perpetuated. Not only did Andrew Chatto constantly urge its submission, even suggesting that Mark Twain accelerate its completion by dictating it into Edison's phonograph instead of writing it out in longhand, but, as I have documented fully in *Mark Twain in England*, Chatto never thought of doctoring the text, and the

THE PRINCE AND THE PAUPER scene from the 1977 film version (20th Century Fox). While disguised as a beggar, the prince finds himself brought before a judge, accused of stealing.

tightness of the publication schedule would not have allowed it in any event. Mark Twain began the rumour by some publicity-raising suggestions that the book was so critical of England as to need expurgation for that market. It was perpetuated after his death by his secretary, Albert Bigelow Paine, printing a letter from the author to the publisher in a form radically different from the text of the letter still on the files of the British publishing house.

In any case, by 1882 Mark Twain was referring to his "most gaudy English income" in royalties, and, in 1887, it attracted the attention of Her Majesty's Inspector of Inland Revenue, who proposed to tax him on it. Clemens at once cheerfully instructed Chatto to pay the money, adding "The country that allows me copyright has the right to tax me" – hardly the view of an Anglophobe. He also extracted the max-

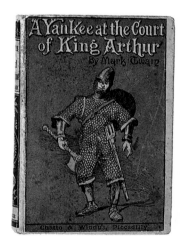

JACKET OF A YANKEE AT THE COURT OF KING ARTHUR (above), published under this title in Britain.

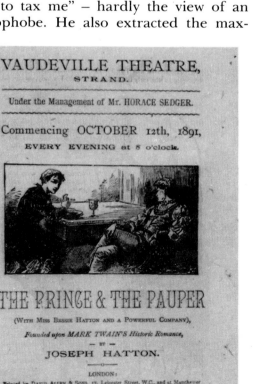

PLAYBILL FOR THE PRINCE AND THE PAUPER (left), produced for the London Stage at the Vaudeville Theatre in 1891.

109

imum fun from the incident in his mock-serious "Petition to the Queen of England" that delighted equally the readers of both countries.

Nevertheless, two years later the *Yankee* made its appearance, his first full-length book in five years since *Huckleberry Finn*. As in that novel, the ending caused him difficulties, but in a different way. Hemingway believed the earlier work ended properly when Jim has been stolen from the boys: "the rest is cheating". There a fundamentally seriously intentioned story degenerates uncomfortably into farce. The *Yankee* begins as farce, modulates into a more sober

work, but ends uncomfortably in a blackness. When little Miss Corbett wrote to Mark Twain he was still thinking of the story as a burlesque. A few months later, writing to Charlie Webster, he complained that the fun had gone out of it, and, much as he wished to, he could not get it back: "I want relief of mind". Evidently he did not achieve that, though some of his subsequent letters imply an occasional, short-lived burst of confidence that it would be both an amusing and an influential book after all.

The comic possibilities in a man from the industrialized America of the final quarter of the nineteenth century finding himself suddenly transposed into the world of King Arthur are obvious. Amused and irritated by the primitiveness, he would want to apply his technological skill to accelerating the pace of progress. This in turn would amaze and terrify the simple people of the sixth century, and that is how the story started out. It quickly became complicated by Mark Twain's change of outlook over the years when the book was in gestation.

The story-line is more complicated than that of *The Prince and the Pauper*, though there are similarities in the questions posed by both. A nineteenth-century visitor to

Warwick Castle encounters a fellow-visitor who is unaccountably familiar with a bullet-hole in a suit of armour which the official guide attributes to later vandalism by Cromwell's troops. The "curious stranger" adds that he made the bullet hole himself, but when the other has recovered from his surprise, the stranger has vanished. In the evening, reading Malory in his hotel room, the first man is again joined by the stranger. The latter, plied with whisky, explains that he was head superintendent in the arms factory at Hartford, Connecticut, who, laid out with a crowbar by an aggrieved work-man, had awakened to find himself in a strange country. He hands to the other a parchment entitled "The Tale of the Lost Land". The text of this forms the main part of the novel.

The Lost Land is, of course, Arthurian England. The newcomer's first and most persistent impression of sixth-century Britain is of its appalling poverty and cruelty. Disturbed by the Yankee's outlandish costume, the authorities threaten him with burning at the stake at noon on the following day. Knowing a total eclipse to be due at that time, the Yankee threatens, if they attempt his execution, to blot out the sun. When the eclipse fulfils this he is immediately released and appointed perpetual minister and executive. Further to demonstrate his superiority over Merlin, he proceeds to astonish the people by blowing up the magician's tower.

This achievement of power through crude superiority of knowledge and know-how characterizes the whole novel. For example, the Yankee's natural and spontaneous lighting of his pipe reduces the frightened knights to further submissiveness. Again, an indication of the broad thrust of the story is more appropriate than precise details of the plot. Once more the picaresque framework of adventures on journeys provides the structure. At first these are comic, ridiculing the artificiality of chivalry (with the occasional predictable aside about Sir Walter Scott) and the clumsiness of armour: where does a knight keep his pocket handkerchief and how does he scratch himself when he itches?

The superstitious respect of the people for the aristocracy, the power of magic, and the Church, forms another butt, as does their general credulity. The Boss, as he is now known (he is later also referred to as Hank Morgan), has acquired as companions a page, Clarence, and a young girl, Sandy. The latter is so indoctrinated with legends and fairy-tales as readily to believe that a herd of swine are really nobles transformed by an enchanter who need to be rescued from enslavement. A more obvious and pernicious form of slavery is evident throughout the land, though, and inevitably this prompts Mark Twain to more serious indictments of man's inhumanity to man and of tyranny in general.

111

THE EFFECTS OF SUN ON ARMOUR *(right): "I was like to get fried in that stove"* (A Yankee at the Court of King Arthur).

THE KING OF AMERICAN HUMOUR *(below right) meets King Edward VII and Queen Alexandra of Great Britain at a Windsor garden party.*

WINDSOR CASTLE *(below), the largest castle in England and a favourite home of the Royal Family.*

This in turn leads to reflections on the inequalities and evils of a monarchical system, and a rigid class structure. Seeking to inject some democracy into the king, the Boss persuades Arthur to join him in disguising themselves as commoners and to see how such people live. This is as educative to Arthur as to the Prince in the earlier novel. One incident, though, restores even the Yankee's flagging faith in human nature, and he concludes:

A man *is* a man at bottom. Whole ages of abuse and oppression cannot crush the manhood clear out of him. Whoever thinks it a mistake is himself mistaken. Yes, there is plenty good enough material for a republic in the most degraded people that ever existed . . . if one could but force it out of its timid and suspicious privacy, to overthrow and trample in the mud any throne that was ever set up and any nobility that ever supported it . . . Yes, there was no occasion to give up my dream yet awhile.

So far, so democratically republican in the American tradition, even though the Boss later admits to wanting to achieve the dream bloodlessly and to become the republic's first president himself: "Yes, there was more or less human nature in me. I found that out." By this stage of the novel the Boss has introduced the populace to the benefits of the nineteenth century – newspapers, education, commercialism, industrialization and taxes. Then there are "The telegraph, the telephone, the phonograph, the type-writer, the sewing machine, and all the thousand willing and handy servants of steam and electricity". Maritime communications have been modernized, and he is "getting ready to send out an expedition to discover America". Knights are being used as commercial travellers or to carry banners advertising particular products, and they go into action on bicycles rather than horses.

All good clean unsophisticated fun, but throughout there has been reiterated emphasis on the poverty, cruelty, violence and credulity prevalent throughout the kingdom. There have been increasing signs of dissidence, stirred up by Merlin and disaffected knights, and not even the Boss's marriage to Sandy and the birth of their daughter can offset the mounting tension. Often as Merlin is outwitted, he always recovers support, and from a temporary absence abroad in the interest of his ailing child's health Hank Morgan returns to find chaos. The Church has forbidden electricity, so the country is in darkness; Arthur has discovered Launcelot's affair with Guenever, but Launcelot has also swindled the King's nephews by manipulating rail-stock in the stock market. This leads to Arthur's last battle in which he and the Round Table knights are killed.

In a last desperate attempt to bring about the republic he dreams of, the Boss challenges the opposition to take on him and fifty-two youths, trained for his standing army at his new West Point academy. Surrounded by electric fences and minefields, and armed with gatling guns, they await the attack. When it comes, nineteenth-century instruments of war, reinforced by an artificially induced flood, kill twenty-five thousand men in ten minutes, and success for the little band seems secured.

That is, until they realize that they have trapped themselves, for the stench from so many rotting corpses is poisoning the air and killing all of them. Clarence provides a postscript in which Merlin, victorious at the last, casts a spell on the Boss, dooming him to sleep for thirteen centuries. This explains his reincarnation in Warwick Castle, and a final postscript, provided by the author, describes pathetically the death of the exhausted old man in the Warwick hotel.

The book presents a problem which has occupied the attention of many critics, notably, in *Mark Twain's Fable of Progress*, Henry Nash Smith, who did so much to foster the best Mark Twain scholarship. The book seems patently designed as a fable, rather than as the burlesque it seems at first sight, but a fable of what? Progress was much in the air at this time in the USA particularly. It was an age of great and rapid development in mechanization, industrialization

and mercantile enterprise. Fortunes were being made in oil, steel, railways and other spheres of new activity, and the names of the great "Captains of Industry", like Andrew Carnegie and John D. Rockefeller, were increasingly prominent, both as entrepreneurs and philanthropic public benefactors, as were bankers such as John Pierpoint Morgan. All of these were men with interests wider than business and extending into more cultural fields. It was an area that fascinated Mark Twain and, as will

WARWICK CASTLE (*above*). *Having visited the castle during one of his English visits, Twain chose to set the beginning of* A Yankee at the Court of King Arthur *there.*

RAGPICKERS' COURT, MULBERRY STREET, NEW YORK (*left*). *In* A Connecticut Yankee at King Arthur's Court *Twain attempted to marry a historical romance with more pointed social comment on the growing gap between rich and poor evident in his own time.*

113

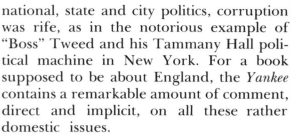

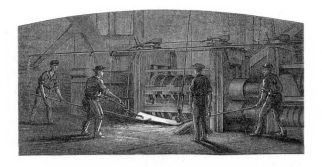

be seen in the next chapter, one in which he had some personal involvement.

The man who popularized the term "Captains of Industry" was Thorstein Veblen, a social scientist and an original thinker with a lively turn of phrase. A decade after the Yankee was published Veblen was to bring out his *Theory of the Leisure Class* in which he identified "conspicuous consumption" as an inevitable concomitant of a business ethic. Put at its simplest, this manifests itself in the acquisition and display of artifacts evident of the owner's wealth but unrelated to his mode of earning a living, articles which demonstrated that he had the money to live in a leisured manner. Mark Twain's Hartford house was in part an early manifestation of this. In the *Yankee* Chapter 32, "Dowley's Humiliation", foreshadows this kind of ostentatious display and the rivalry and one-upmanship it engenders.

It was also a period of great venality. *The Gilded Age* had not eradicated that in politics or elsewhere, but, though the age survived, its gilt was becoming distinctly tarnished. Panics on the stock exchange were often the result of shady dealings like those attributed to Launcelot, and if fortunes were made, they were as quickly lost. So too in national, state and city politics, corruption was rife, as in the notorious example of "Boss" Tweed and his Tammany Hall political machine in New York. For a book supposed to be about England, the *Yankee* contains a remarkable amount of comment, direct and implicit, on all these rather domestic issues.

A decade before that book, the American economist, Henry George, had, in the title of his best-known work, summarized its theme and pointed to another disturbing feature of this opulence: *Progress and Poverty*. His thesis was that industrial and commercial progress brought great increases of wealth, but great increases in poverty were an inescapable concomitant. George Bernard Shaw would claim that it was Henry George whose views converted him to anti-capitalistic socialism. If George did not have so dramatic an effect on his compatriot, Samuel Clemens, he must nevertheless have found in *The Prince and the Pauper* and in the *Yankee* encouraging evidence that his ideas were gaining hold.

In addition to all this, the age was still adjusting nervously to the implications of Darwinism, as it was popularly conceived. Meanwhile, social philosophers like the Englishman Herbert Spencer were boldly applying Darwinian principles to society and producing an evolutionary theory of social Darwinism. Heretical as many people found all these notions, they were current throughout the Western world, and Mark Twain was far from unique in his confusion when trying to hold them all in balance.

Stylistically, as well as intellectually, this confusion is amply evident in the book. Half a century ago one influential American critic argued that "it was in consequence of pursuing his humorous writing that he was arrested in his moral and aesthetic development". This is too facile, and indeed it is the humour that is more seriously arrested by the moral indignation and despair that ends the novel in that holocaust. Nor can the *Yankee* be readily classified as fusing humour and moral concern in the acceptable literary form of satire. Clemens once observed, "Byron despised the human race because he despised himself. I feel as Byron did and for the same reason." If you despise yourself and the race, you do not write "The Vision of Judgment", for beneath the contempt that poem displays for monarchs, hypocrites, and poetasters lies a strongly positive belief in liberty and in the potential of man to choose liberty. The satirist is usually the idealist in disguise.

Mark Twain recognised that fact in his 1879 comment that, to succeed, satire must spring from "a calm judicial good humor". If anger is necessary, he might have added, it must be a controlled, directed anger, and not his own tendency "to curse and foam at the mouth". Nor is he always clear as to exactly what it is that he is satirising. For instance, at one point Hank and the King are irritated by the smith, Dowley, who boasts of the luxuries with which his house is furnished. A chapter title, "Dowley's Humiliation", promises to anticipate Veblen in its attack on so blatant an example of conspicuous consumption. In fact, the Yankee merely outsmarts Dowley by producing an instantaneous display of even more conspicuous forms of consumption, just as, in the next chapter, he defeats Dowley in a discussion on political economy less by argument than by the fortuitous advantage of nineteenth-century hindsight on a sixth-century problem.

In *Gulliver's Travels* Swift satirizes human nature by arguing that it is despicable, but if Swift does not totally convince us of the innate and irredeemable depravity of man it is because of the attractiveness of Gulliver himself: there must be hope for a race that can produce even one Gulliver. Mark Twain, an apostle of progress, sets out ostensibly to satirize what he sees as bad in the outworn creeds of Arthurian Britain, but no character in the book is big enough to sustain his belief in progress. The Yankee is smarter than Dowley, but he is not better in any absolute sense; he may be self-sufficient, but he lacks self-knowledge. The enormous progress in scientific and technological know-how in which the novel glories is unmatched by any corresponding development in the moral nature of man. Though that development is on occasion asserted, the whole thrust of the fable seems to belie it:

There is no such thing as nature; what we call by that misleading name is merely heredity and training. We have no thoughts of our own; they are transmitted to us, trained into us.

This line of social Darwinism is self-defeating in a book on progress, denying, as it does, any autonomous choice to man. Clemens was, at this time, struggling within himself to reconcile a belief in progress with an awareness of moral poverty, much as Henry George was to try to reconcile it with an awareness of economic poverty. There is a Tennysonian dimension to this, except that Clemens seems unable even to adopt Tennyson's evasive solution and to "stretch lame hands of faith,/And faintly trust the larger hope". T.S. Eliot remarked of Tennyson that "Temperamentally, he was opposed to the doctrine that he was moved to accept and praise." He sees Tennyson not as the frustrated artist but as the frustrated moralist: "I should reproach Tenny-

MOULE'S MAP OF NINETEENTH-
CENTURY LONDON *(right)*,
*showing the four Counties of
Surrey, Kent, Essex and
Middlesex, which then extended
right into the city.*

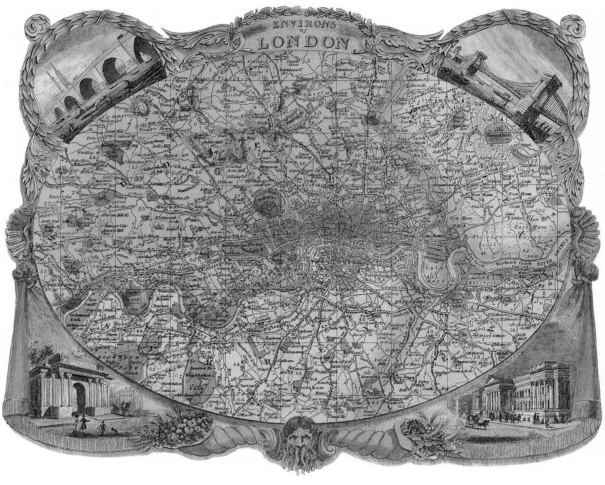

*MARK TWAIN IN 1909 (right)
seated on the terrace of his last
home, "Stormfield", an Italianate
villa set on a hilltop at Redding,
Connecticut.*

son not for mildness, or tepidity, but rather for lack of serenity". Perhaps the problem with *A Connecticut Yankee at King Arthur's Court* is that Mark Twain too had insufficiently acquired that quality which he had admired in Judge Oliver, and which he thought to have found, many years earlier, in the European way of life.

Perhaps, also, he expected too much of the book. The story that Chatto had had to modify it for the English public may have originated in the author's wish to see it taken as satirical social comment in a way that his own reputation as a humorist and the sheer enjoyable fun of so much of the book prevented. In Britain some reviewers deplored the vulgarization of the Arthurian legend, preferring Tennyson's treatment of it, but the book was not seen as the savage attack on royalty that Clemens wanted it to be. He must have had mixed feelings when Chatto, with characteristic dryness, reported to him an enquiry from "a Russian publisher for whom Siberia seems to have no terrors". The only change Chatto made was "keeping the title to your original wording, *A Yankee at the Court of King Arthur*, which is shorter and I think more easily grasped by the British public". Under either title, it is still capable of giving considerable pleasure and some worthwhile food for thought.

A Tramp Abroad
More Tramps Abroad
Joan of Arc
The Mysterious Stranger

MARK TWAIN AND THE WORLD

Except for one brief retrospect, the chronological and geographical threads of this narrative now come together in the final twenty years of Samuel Clemens's life. The tone of his writings after 1890 is foreshadowed in the pessimism of *A Connecticut Yankee*. It is at its best in *The Tragedy of Pudd'nhead Wilson*, his last major full-length novel, and such attempts at sustained humour as survived in his work seem strained and tired by comparison with his earlier exuberance. Eventually he succumbed, in *The Mysterious Stranger*, to a nihilistic blackness so total that the story was never published until 1922, twelve years after his death.

One attempt at reviving his earlier success looked promising when *The American Claimant* was announced to appear in 1892, for the claimant of the title was to be Colonel Sellers, whose comic eccentricities had popularized *The Gilded Age* as novel and play. *The American Claimant* reworked some of the material Clemens and Howells had earlier made into the unsuccessful play usually known as *Colonel Sellers as a Scientist*, although "The American Claimant" had actually been considered as an alternative title. Unfortunately, reincarnated in the 1892 context, Sellers requires a much greater "willing suspension of disbelief" to be remotely credible. His schemes and the whole plot are crudely far-fetched, and the interest in the psychology of claimants and problems of identity that Mark Twain had developed in the interim is certainly not employed effectively here. Comedy had lapsed regrettably into farce.

Yet the basic idea was promising: an English nobleman's heir, wishing to try making his own way and his own fortune in America, proposes that his father should hand over the estates to the American claimant rather than to him. It should have provided Mark Twain with an ideal vehicle for the comparison and contrast of the two cultures that so much of his own experience had qualified him so eminently to draw. Yet for once the man whose earlier reputation

MARK TWAIN, *1907 (opposite), wearing one of the white suits which, he said, made him "the only cleanly clothed human being in all Christendom north of the Tropics".*

CAPTAIN STORMFIELD'S VISIT TO HEAVEN (left). Extracts from this novel by Twain were published in Harper's in 1907 and 1908 before the book appeared in 1909. First conceived decades before its publication, it is a deliberate debunking of military glory.

had been built on his ability to transmute personal experience into a vividly vernacular literature, relevant to the concerns of his own times, prefers a turgid, conventional narrative crammed with improbabilities and coincidence, where mistaken identity and role-reversal produce only limp and laboured humour.

Other revivals of characters who had been popular in earlier books, and the number of projects begun and abandoned in his last twenty years, suggest a flagging of the creative imagination. *Tom Sawyer Abroad* (subtitled "by Huck Finn edited by Mark Twain"), was published in 1894: in it Tom, with Huck and Jim, becomes accidentally involved in a flight by balloon to various parts of the world, but again the plot is far-fetched, the fun relatively puerile, and, despite the topicality of flight and Clemens's interest in travel, another opportunity is missed. Two years later *Tom Sawyer, Detective*, again narrated by Huck, and this time firmly located in the South, is little better, and certainly comes nowhere near to adapting a story of detection to the more subtle use that he had found for it in *Pudd'nhead Wilson*. Between 1891 and 1902 he began, and laid aside, several attempts to re-utilize the two boys: one plot, in his mind for some years, envisaged them in frontier territory having adventures with the Indians; in another they are becoming aware of a discreetly nascent sexuality, while a potentially more promising idea would have taken them as sexagenarians back to Hannibal where they were to die together.

Yet more than flagging creativity is evident in all this. The fun had gone out of his life as it was going out of his fiction. The Hartford house, much as he loved it, was a constant financial burden to him. Its upkeep demanded more money than his books were bringing in, and he had tried to augment that by dramatizations. *The Prince and the Pauper* was an obvious possibility and in 1884 his own version had widened his family's range of amateur theatricals, but was not substantial enough to justify professional production.

By 1889 there were two adaptations by other people, one of which (by Daniel Froh-

man and Abby Sage Richardson) opened on Christmas Eve in Philadelphia and ran with some success in New York, only to lead to an application for an injunction by one of Clemens's old friends, Edward H. House, who claimed that he had received from Clemens the rights of dramatization several years earlier. The injunction was granted after a lengthy public hearing, which damaged Mark Twain's reputation considerably. That source of revenue was closed, and House joined the lengthening list of ex-friends who Clemens felt had betrayed him. In London, however, the indefatigable Chatto managed successfully to insist on a production of the alternative dramatization, by Mrs Beringer, at the Gaiety Theatre, on the grounds that, under English copyright law, he, as publisher of the novel, was "the only person who can authorize the dramatization of it in this Country". Another version, rewritten by Joseph Hutton, opened at the Vaudeville Theatre, London, in October 1891.

By the 1890s Clemens's business ventures were not doing well. Charles L. Webster & Co. continued in existence, although Webster himself had been encouraged into retirement in 1888 by his disillusioned employer who, for the rest of his life, would blame Webster vitriolically for many of the disasters that assailed him. Over his successor, Fred Hall, Clemens exercised a much closer supervision but the many distractions besetting himself still contributed to errors and confusions for which he blamed Hall. Chatto and his colleagues gave long-distance advice and support, but even their efforts were unable to secure for Webster & Co. the autobiographical work by Stanley, the explorer, with which Clemens had hoped to follow up *The Personal Memoirs of General Grant*, the *Autobiography of Henry Ward Beecher* and other successes.

The coup by which in the 1880s he had obtained Grant's book, though, had led to litigation, and the marketing of the book had led to more, all of which ate into the profits, but what troubled him also had been the personal vilification of himself in the press. He complained once of having gained the reputation in the newspapers of being "the craftiest & most unscrupulous business-sharp in the country". Nevertheless the success of the *Memoirs* had led him

into over-extending his resources dangerously in further publishing ventures.

An even bigger worry was the Paige Typesetting Machine, the project into which his fascination with mechanization, invention and business enterprise had led him as early as 1881 to invest $5,000. By the 1890s he had poured in many thousands more to meet an inevitable series of teething troubles, but it was at last becoming disconcertingly apparent that Paige's machine might not be the equal of Mergenthaler's Linotype, an invention ten years younger. With obstinate loyalty Clemens still followed his hunch financially rather

MARK TWAIN (*above*), *a portrait painted in oil by Isaac Rader over a photograph taken in 1903 by Boston photographer Thomas E. Marr at Quarry Farm.*

121

ANDREW CHATTO (*above*), *chairman of the British firm which effectively acted as Twain's agent as well as publishing his books.*

SIR HENRY STANLEY (*below right*), *photographed by John Fergus.*

THE PAIGE TYPESETTER (*below*) *was patented in 1895. Twain invested, and lost, a small fortune in this machine, firmly believing that it would make him into a millionaire.*

than heeding caution. Disaster was to strike him personally even before Mergenthaler bought Paige out in 1897.

As early as 1891 his financial position led him to conclude that it would be economically sensible to move the family abroad for a period. Livy's health, always delicate, provided a convenient explanation for the decision, but in reality it was the cost of upkeep of the house in Hartford: that had to be reduced if there was to be any hope of repaying the creditors. It was closed down, emptied, and the staff dismissed. Though he could not foresee it, an era in the Clemenses' family life ended when they left it in June for Europe.

His fondness for, and popularity in, Germany made that a natural choice, as well as providing opportunities for them to seek, in the popular spa towns, a palliative for his wife's and his own rheumatism. Although they dined once with the Kaiser, they tried to live frugally for a time, but soon the need to keep up appearances commensurate with the attention paid to him by the European public reasserted itself. They moved to Florence, where they lived even more ostentatiously.

Despite all these activities and anxieties, Mark Twain was still desperately writing. He undertook, alone except for a steersman, a trip down the Rhône in a raft-like vessel, in the hope partly of recapturing the romance of his lost past, partly of collecting material for newspaper articles to lead to a book to be called *The Innocents Adrift*. A decade later it was still unfinished, though a version of what he had completed, abridged by Albert Bigelow Paine, was published after Clemens's death with the less evocative title of "Down the Rhône". Books already mentioned, *Tom Sawyer Abroad* and *Pudd'nhead Wilson*, together with *Those Extraordinary Twins*, were written in Europe, though he had completed *The American Claimant* before leaving the US. In Berlin he translated into English the popular German children's book, *Struwwelpeter*, but Fred Hall could not meet the tight publishing schedule Clemens wanted in order to meet the Christmas trade, so that too appeared only posthumously.

There are literary and personal reasons for the change of tone apparent in his work at this time. His wish to be regarded as a serious writer as well as a humorist has been noted already: by the 1890s, with some sixty years behind him, packed with an unusual variety of experience and diminishing optimism, that need seems to have become more urgent. He was calling his religious beliefs, never strictly orthodox, increasingly into question, but a faith in some shred of goodness in human nature had not been totally extinguished even in the Yankee. This he determined to put into what he

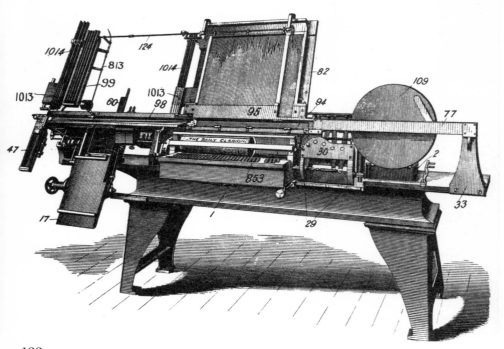

intended as, and always considered, his most valuable contribution to literature, *Personal Recollections of Joan of Arc*, published in 1896. Sadly, and with an irony that would have confirmed his pessimism, it is now probably the least regarded and the least read of his works, and that not merely because hagiography is less to the modern taste than it used to be.

To avoid prejudiced reaction to the work, he originally intended it to be published anonymously. He weakened only to the extent of keeping his familiar pen-name off the title-page, where the text is attributed to "the Sieur Louis de Conte" and described as "Freely translated out of the Ancient French into Modern English from the original unpublished manuscript in the National Archives of France by Jean Francois Alden". Alden and de Conte are transparent pseudonyms, but for the reader who has seen the name of Mark Twain on the binding, the book's seriousness is attested to by the flyleaf listing of eleven "Authorities examined in verification of the truthfulness of this narrative". A "Translator's Preface" is pure panegyric: Joan "occupies the loftiest place possible to human attainment, a loftier one than has been reached by any other mere mortal"; "She was perhaps the

THE CLEMENS CHILDREN *(above)*, *Susy, Jean and Clara. Although his works are read by people of all ages with equal enjoyment, Twain hoped that his historical novels would entertain and inform children in particular. He dedicated* The Prince and the Pauper *to his daughters Susy and Clara.*

JOAN OF ARC *(left). In* The Personal Recollections of Joan of Arc. *Twain tried to correct the image of himself as a humorist by writing a sentimental account of the medieval heroine.*

THE CLEMENS CHILDREN, SUSY
AND CLARA *(above), Onteora,
New York, 1890. This was the
last year of family life together in
the United States. In 1891
Twain was forced to move to
Europe in an attempt to reduce
his living expenses.*

author of *Personal Recollections of Joan of Arc*
was very much more gratifying to her,
believing as she did that her father, by
writing it, had assured for himself a place in
the hall of worthwhile literary fame. Clemens, of course, was silently modelling Joan
on this favourite among his daughters, and
even allowing the writing of the book to
distract him from his business worries: "it
furnished me seven times the pleasure
afforded me by any of the others".

It can only be called a "worthy" book: its
piety consorts strangely with most of his
other published work and is perhaps best
thought of as therapeutically intended, a
final attempt to convince himself of human
goodness, though the story, from that point
of view, is conveniently ambivalent, ending
as it does with the rejection and death of the
heroine at the hands of those she has tried
to help. The writing is undistinguished, the
romantic, sentimental idealization of Joan
extreme even by the standards of its times,
and one almost wishes Clemens had lived
long enough to see how a humorist with
whom he is sometimes compared, George
Bernard Shaw, could handle the same subject. For Shaw, too, it seemed an unlikely
one, yet his is a lighter touch, skilfully
blending respect with a more down-to-earth
attitude. Shaw's Joan is sensibly humanized,
where Mark Twain's is unhealthily idolized.

There is, however, some evidence that
Personal Recollections of Joan of Arc pleased
the contemporary taste in Britain at a time
when there was considerable interest in her.
Her beatification (achieved in 1909) was
already under discussion. (She was not
canonized until 1920.) She was the subject
of a verse drama by the Manxman, J.H.
Skrine; the popular Scottish novelist, Margaret Oliphant, had published a book on
her, and so had another Scot, the eminent
poet, scholar and critic, Andrew Lang.
Lang had been a staunch champion and
admirer of Mark Twain, even publishing a
poem on him for his fiftieth birthday.
However, the Yankee proved, in Huck's
phrase, "too many for him", and Lang
wrote a very severe review of it.

Although Lang's own expertise enabled
him to point to certain anachronisms and
inaccuracies in *Joan of Arc*, and he considers
Clemens had made her "too much like an
argumentative young 'school-ma'am' ", his

only entirely unselfish person whose name
has a place in profane history", a "noble
child, the most innocent, the most lovely,
the most adorable the ages have produced".
A further "Translator's Note" italicizes the
statement that hers is "the only story of a
human life which comes to us under oath".
In short, *Joan of Arc* is a classic product of
what, in the title of the first essay I published on this author, I called *Mark Twain
the Great Victorian*.

His independently minded daughter
Susy, by then a student at Bryn Mawr, often
found it embarrassing, like the daughters of
other famous men, to be known primarily
for her parentage, but – in this respect,
more her mother's daughter – she was
particularly sensitive about her kinship to
the humorist "Mark Twain" and came to
hate that name. To be the daughter of the

TWAIN IN 1908 *(left)*, *the year he moved to his new home, "Stormfield", in Redding, Connecticut.*

review of that book was more sympathetic and constructive than might have been expected. Mark Twain's use of Joan's page as the narrator Lang sees as an effective parallel to the role of Huck; he also likes Mark Twain's attribution to Joan of "American humour throughout, and not so very remote from the medieval". He is perhaps a little harsh in finding that the "dialogue is Mississippian; the historic sense of time and manners is absent", but he recognizes that Mark Twain's "heart is in it", praising the book as "honest, spirited, and stirring" and likely to extend American interest in Joan. Sir Walter Besant, novelist and social reformer, writing in the ladies' weekly, *The Queen*, commended Mark Twain's "most moving portraiture" of Joan as "more spiritual, of a loftier type than we could have conceived possible in the author of 'Huckleberry Finn'", adding unctuously that the book proved Clemens to have "a nature or a soul . . . lifted high above the common run". At last, in Britain at least, Mark Twain had achieved his ambition to be taken seriously.

WALL STREET, NEW YORK *(left)*, *nineteenth-century engraving from* Harper's Magazine. *The financial crisis of 1893–94, which resulted in the failure of business all over the United States, forced Twain into voluntary bankruptcy.*

Even while he was finishing the book the catastrophe that was to shatter any residual optimism was about to explode. In January 1895 he completed both *Tom Sawyer, Detective* and *Joan of Arc* in a state of understandable exhaustion, aggravated by frequent solitary crossings and re-crossings of the Atlantic since 1892 to attend to business problems, sometimes being away from Livy for months on end. Webster & Co. was more desperately over-extended than ever, having rashly committed itself, with Clemens's consent, to the publication of a massive ten-volume Library of American Literature (it later became eleven) edited by E.C. Stedman, a poet, essayist and critic of some distinction, as well as a Wall Street broker. His friendship with Mark Twain had included advising him on the manuscript of the *Yankee*, but that did not prevent his quickly becoming, in Clemens's view, another ex-friend to be reviled for having let him down.

The Paige typesetter, though technically much improved, could not be put into production for lack of capital to set up the necessary manufacturing company, and because of Paige's objections to the idea. Then another Wall Street crash in June 1893 brought ruin to businesses, banks and railway companies by the score. Not only was it impossible to sell off Webster & Co., Clemens could not even raise the money to pay off its debts. At the eleventh hour salvation

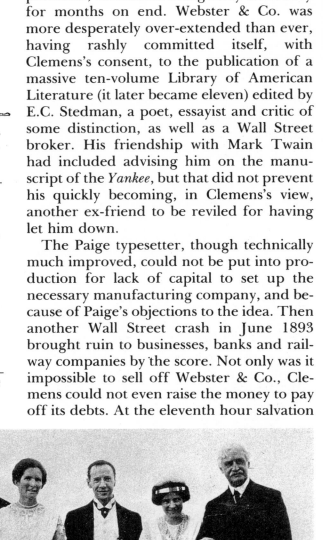

loomed in the improbable shape of Henry Huttleston Rogers, well known as a ruthless business man, a trustee of the Standard Oil Trust, and an archetypal robber baron of the kind at which Mark Twain had tilted in the *Yankee*. (One of Dan Beard's many inspired illustrations for that book, "The Slave-driver", is said to have been unmistakably modelled on the features of another of the breed, Jay Gould, entrepreneur, railway magnate and ally of "Boss" Tweed.) Unlike Gould, however, Rogers had a gift for friendship and was a firm admirer of Mark Twain's writings. Producing large injections of cash, he seemed to have staved off the disaster facing both the publishing house and the typesetter, but, more important, he became friend, financial adviser and confidant to Clemens for the rest of his life.

Not even Rogers could fend off trouble indefinitely. Unemployment and poverty still infested the streets of New York and other cities, and Mark Twain was becoming a connoisseur of irony. First, the typesetter he thought "Very much the best investment I have ever made" had ruined him; second, he had to accept help from one of the men he had been so vigorously condemning from *The Gilded Age* onwards; third, against the background of the collapse of his private finances, his reputation was now soaring and he was being fêted in opulent New York clubs, restaurants and apartments, as well as in Boston, where a copy of *Huckleberry Finn* had once been publicly burnt. Yale University had already given him an Honorary MA in 1888. *Pudd'nhead Wilson*, being serialized in the *Century* before publication in book form (it had brought him an invaluable $6,500 for the serial rights), was winning the plaudits of writers as eminent as Oliver Wendell Holmes.

Eventually, in February 1895, the affairs of Webster & Co. degenerated to the point where even Rogers advised voluntary bankruptcy. Clemens accepted, but another irony still awaited him. In determining that he would, by his own literary efforts, earn enough money to pay off his creditors in full as soon as possible, he was emulating an earlier major writer facing that identical disaster – Sir Walter Scott. Aspects of Scott he had always admired, and doubtless he took pride in proving himself Scott's equal in honour (one hesitates to invoke chivalry), as he had done in popularity and literary stature, showing that an American would not be outdone by a Briton.

To implement this, he turned inevitably to a tried standby: another travel book. His last had been *A Tramp Abroad* in 1880, based on his tour with Joe Twichell (fictionalized, and used humorously, as Mr Harris). Mark Twain himself masquerades at times as a painter in oils and a collector of ceramics, as well as, more credibly, a student of the German language. Chapter I takes them

THE AUTHOR'S MEMORIES *(opposite right) of his European tour in 1878 provided the basis for* A Tramp Abroad, *published in 1880.*

A STREET IN CHAMONIX *(left):* "*Never did a mountain seem so close; its big sides seemed at one's very elbow, and its majestic dome, and the lofty cluster of slender minarets that were its neighbours, seemed to be almost over one's head*" (A Tramp Abroad).

COVER OF *A TRAMP ABROAD (below left), Twain's most successful book since* The Innocents Abroad.

"WE HAD SLEPT AN HOUR AND A HALF AND MISSED ALL THE SCENERY!" *(below). After a good dinner, the travellers fall asleep during the drive to Meiringen* (A Tramp Abroad).

SIX VIEWS OF SWITZERLAND *(right). Swiss lithographs of 1830 show the Lake at Lucerne (top left), the Jungfrau from Interlaken (top right), the glacier and village of Argentière (centre left), le Jardin at Chamonix (centre right), the lake of Geneva (bottom left), and the castle at Chillon (bottom right), all of which were visited by the narrator of* A Tramp Abroad.

"A YAWN OF SUCH COMPREHENSIVENESS" *(below) "that the bulk of her face disappears behind her upper lip, and one is able to see how she is constructed inside" (A Tramp Abroad).*

from Hamburg, through Frankfort-am-Main, to Heidelberg, where the next eighteen chapters are based (including a lengthy excursion on the Neckar by raft, which in some respects anticipates the idyllic aspects of *Huckleberry Finn*). Thence to Baden-Baden, for four chapters, and on to Switzerland, visiting Lucerne, Interlaken, the Alps, Zermatt, Chamonix and Geneva in the course of twenty-three chapters, the last of which also includes Turin. Then a chapter each on Milan and Venice, and a final chapter on art in Rome and Florence with thoughts on "the fig-leaf mania" that

work up the notebook material referred to in my previous chapter.

By covering less ground geographically than *The Innocents Abroad, A Tramp Abroad* is able to deal more fully with the places visited, though the rapid dismissal of Italy at the end suggests a careless allocation of space or, perhaps (more generously), the recollection that Italy had been dealt with in the earlier book. That consideration, however, does not prevent some duplication, as in yet another account of the Castle of Chillon. *A Tramp Abroad* adopts a discursive, rambling, anecdotal style, similar to its predecessor's, but handles it rather better. There is the same naive fun to be extracted from the foreignness of Europeans, the same alternation between serious description and derisively comic versions of legends and traditions. The viewpoint is still that of "the boys", in its philistine scepticism of art and aesthetes, but whereas in *The Innocents Abroad* the target was primarily the Old Masters, this time the narrator is prepared to take on his contemporaries. He ridicules the boring artificiality of opera, especially Wagner's, and of the Turner cult in painting; the description, in Chapter XXIV, of his "conversion" to an appreciation of Turner's "Slave Ship" by Mr Ruskin, who "is educated in art", is a more sophisticated piece of irony than he was capable of in the 1870 book, though the humour elsewhere is often as unsophisticated.

The book is probably most remembered, with justice, by modern readers for two elements: Jim Baker's Blue Jay Yarn and Appendix D, "The Awful German Language". The former is an anecdote from Clemens's *Roughing It* days, comparable in narrative skill to the Judge Oliver anecdote in *The Innocents Abroad* – and hardly more directly relevant to the subject of the book. The other is Mark Twain at his humorous best: irreverent, hilarious, but grounded in a genuine knowledge of and interest in the subject. Where his usual method is to make the extravagantly fanciful sound real, here he makes the real sound extravagantly fanciful, yet, cut through the humour and there are worse ways of introducing the serious student to the actual pitfalls of the German language. The student of Mark Twain has the added advantage, here perhaps more than anywhere, of imagining himself listening to the poker-faced, drawling Mark Twain of the lecture platform in such instances as this example of the illogical genders of nouns: "In German a young lady has no sex, while a turnip has. Think what overwrought reverence that shows for the turnip, and what callous disrespect for the girl."

Lavishly and amusingly illustrated by a team of artists that even included the author himself, the book's reputation was rapidly established. By 1907 Chatto alone had published 175,000 copies, and at the beginning it was also pirated in Britain.

A CHILD SAVED *(left)*: "*we thought she was gone, sure, for the ground slanted steeply, and to save herself seemed a sheer impossibility; but she managed to scramble up, and ran by us laughing*" (A Tramp Abroad).

A CARAVAN FROM ZERMATT *(above)*: "*When the procession stood at ease, roped together, and ready to move, I never saw a finer sight. It was 3,122 feet long*" (A Tramp Abroad).

Tauchnitz did well with it in Europe, as did Bliss in America. Yet, though it was lucrative, Mark Twain found the writing of it tedious drudgery. Despite that, in the dark days of 1895, this was once more the characteristically masochistic method he settled on for raising money. But what territory to explore this time?

He had written himself out on Europe, even if his exile there had not over-exposed him to its attractions. His Western experience lay too far in the past, and interest in the West was waning. (It was in 1893 that Frederick Jackson Turner lectured to the American Historical Association in Chicago on *The Significance of the Frontier in American History* and officially announced the disappearance of the Frontier with the end of westward expansion.) New regions would

RICHARD WAGNER *(below). Of his visit to the opera in Mannheim to see* Lohengrin, *Twain wrote, "The racking and pitiless pain of it remains stored up in my memory alongside the memory of the time that I had my teeth fixed" (*A Tramp Abroad*).*

THE PLACE D'IENA, *Paris (below). It was while Twain was living in Paris in 1894 that he conceived the idea of a travel book based on a trip around the world.*

have to be visited, sick of travel as he was. The advantages were also occurring to him, in the interests of ready cash, of combining that travel with a well-paid lecture tour but, popular as his works had become in translation, a lecture tour required an English-speaking audience.

The two ideas coalesced in a topical, if over-ambitious scheme: a trip round the world could be accomplished entirely within continental America and the British Empire. Jules Verne's *Around the World in Eighty Days* had been popular for twenty years, the quatercentenary of Columbus's discovery of the New World had been celebrated in 1892: why not circumnavigate and talk your way round the English-speaking world, especially when you were already a living legend there? Moreover, with the Frontier closed, America was turning to more imperialistic policies: the British Empire would be worth a critical inspection for the lessons it might offer.

Ending his European exile to return from Paris to Elmira before setting out on the world tour, he regarded Paris as its starting point. This would enable him to end the circumnavigation at Southampton and recuperate quietly in England while he wrote it up.

Accompanied by Olivia and Clara, their eldest daughter (Jean and Susy, the younger ones, were to remain in the States), he left Elmira on 14 July 1895 (reminding himself, perhaps, that it was Bastille Day in France, but his self-imposed sentence was only beginning). He started lecturing in Cleveland, Ohio, and moved westward as far as Vancouver, making twenty-two appearances on the lecturing platform. In the rest of the trip he gave about another hundred and ten: the $30,000 in fees that he remitted to Rogers represented between a third and a half of the total debt. He had an offer of $10,000 from his American publisher for the book, and he himself had ideas of serialisation, as well as English publication. Paying off his debts might well be within his reach, but at a price.

Although he was only sixty when he left, he felt much older. Life expectancy was shorter in those days, but it was not that. His health had been poor for some years, he had had too much worry, too much overwork, too much expatriation, and too much travel. He needed the spell of quiet domestic rest that his pattern of life had never allowed him, and the last thing he really wanted was the enormous journey with which he had saddled himself. At least the short stay at Elmira had improved his health to some extent: he joked that "There is more Clemens than carbuncle now".

From Victoria, British Columbia, their
itinerary took them to Australia, pausing at
Honolulu and the Fiji Islands. After Sydney
they went on to Melbourne, thence to Ade-
laide, Queensland, Ballarat, and finally
Bendigo. New Zealand followed, via
Hobart, Tasmania: they reached Bluff and
Dunedin early in November. Then Gis-
borne and Nelson, returning to Sydney to
take ship for Ceylon. On to India: Bombay,
Allahabad, Calcutta, Cawnpore, the Taj
Mahal, Lahore, Delhi, Madras, and so to
Mauritius. Finally, South Africa: Durban,
Johannesburg, Cape Town, and back via

OVERFLOWING OF THE BANK OF STRUPERMADER (above), aquatint by Lieutenant James Hunter, c. 1904. From Australia Twain went to India, where he arrived in January 1886.

KILLADER'S TOMB, OUSCOTTAH (right), aquatint by Lieutenant James Hunter, c. 1904.

CECIL RHODES (1853–1902) (right), portrait by William Nicholson, 1900. Financier and statesman, Rhodes was prime minister of the Cape Colony of South Africa at the time of Twain's world tour.

SOUTH AFRICA (far right). Chinese workers sign on to work in the mines.

Madeira to Southampton at last, on 31 July 1896, thirteen months after leaving there for Elmira.

Eagerly awaiting the arrival of the two daughters, Jean and Susy, whom they had not seen in that period, they settled temporarily at Guildford, within reach of London and Andrew Chatto, who had become, in effect, their British agent. In mid-August news came that the departure of the girls from the States was delayed by the illness of Susy. Olivia and Clara immediately set off for Hartford; Clemens waited in agony alone in Surrey. His isolation, and his dependence on his publisher as a friend, is touchingly evidenced. A letter to Olivia, saying that he thought Chatto was on holiday, ends with an underlined postscript: "Chatto has come!" There is no more information on that meeting, but it was clearly not devoted exclusively to royalty negotiations on the new book.

Then, as if he had not already suffered enough, on the next day the telegram he dreaded arrived: before Olivia and Clara had had time to reach New York, his favourite daughter had died of meningitis at the age of twenty-four. He may be forgiven if, after all his travels, he recalled the lines from Coleridge's "Ancient Mariner":

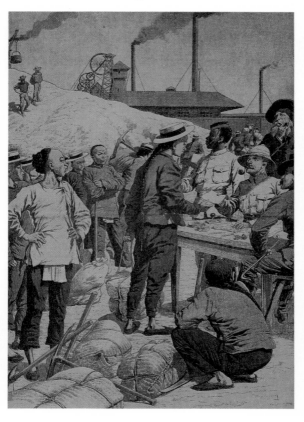

"This man hath penance done/And penance more shall do". How unforeseeably right he had been, facing ruin in 1894, to write, with intended irony, to tell his wife, "Cheer up, the worst is yet to come". The albatross of guilt that he had hung round his own neck all his life would now, unlike the one in Coleridge, never dislodge itself. Susy's death he would always see as a punishment for sins he could not really believe he had committed. At the beginning of the '90s his daughters, almost adult, admitted that they had sometimes found his moods frightening, and that had been enough to awaken in him unintended paroxysms of self-torment. For his brother Henry's accidental death in the steamboat accident of 1858 he still considered himself responsible. Now his conscience was loaded with the burden of another death.

Early in September the surviving members of the family were reunited in Guildford. Deciding to settle in London for a while, they sought Chatto's advice on suitable areas, eventually agreeing on a house in a quiet part of Chelsea, 23 Tedworth Square. Recognizing work as the only anodyne for grief, Clemens settled down to writing. By 24 October 1896 the first chapter of a book provisionally entitled "Round

MARK TWAIN, *in 1907 (above).*

the World" was finished and Chatto was told that Clemens would accept no lecture engagements. His heart was never in the book, but by March he had completed the manuscript. He had returned to the American Publishing Company, now run by Elisha Bliss's son, Frank, who was told in mid-March "I have set the type-writer to

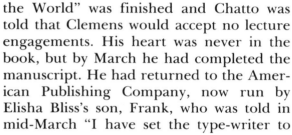

GUILDFORD HIGH STREET (*left*), *photographed c. 1860. Twain was staying in Guildford in a rented house when he learnt that his favourite daughter Susy had died of meningitis.*

133

PAGE 596 OF *MORE TRAMPS ABROAD* (right), undated holograph. The British version of Twain's book about his round-the-world travels was set from the manuscript by Chatto. The note on this page shows Chatto querying a cricket statistic which was subsequently re-worded in the English text (see facing page).

PAGE 216 OF *FOLLOWING THE EQUATOR* (far right), the shorter American version of the same work, was published by the American Publishing Company in 1897. It retained Twain's wording of the phrase in question.

596

Mr. Chauncy once saw "a little native man" throw a cricket-ball 119 yards. This is said to beat the English professional record by 13 yards. (29th *Whitaker's Almanac*)

We have all seen the circus-man bound into the air from a spring-board & make a summer-sault over eight horses standing side by side. Mr. Chauncy saw an aboriginal do it over [crossed out] eleven; & was assured that he had some times done it over four-teen. But what is that to this:

"I saw the same man leap from the ground, & in going over he dipped his head, unaided by his hands, into a hat placed in an inverted position on the top of the head of another man sitting upright on horseback — both man & horse being of the average

216   FOLLOWING THE EQUATOR.

dead — in the body; but he has features that will live in literature.

Mr. Philip Chauncy, an officer of the Victorian Government, contributed to its archives a report of his personal observations of the aboriginals which has in it some things which I wish to condense slightly and insert here. He speaks of the quickness of their eyes and the accuracy of their judgment of the direction of approaching missiles as being quite extraordinary, and of the answering suppleness and accuracy of limb and muscle in avoiding the missile as being extraordinary also. He has seen an aboriginal stand as a target for cricket-balls thrown with great force ten or fifteen yards, by professional bowlers, and successfully dodge them or parry them with his shield during about half an hour. One of those balls, properly placed, could have killed him; "Yet he depended, with the utmost self-possession, on the quickness of his eye and his agility."

The shield was the customary war-shield of his race, and would not be a protection to you or to me. It is no broader than a stovepipe, and is about as long as a man's arm. The opposing surface is not flat, but slopes away from the center-line like a boat's bow. The difficulty about a cricket-ball that has been thrown with a scientific "twist" is, that it suddenly changes it course when it is close to its target and comes straight for the mark when apparently it was going overhead or to one side. I should not be able to protect myself from such balls for half-an-hour, or less.

Mr. Chauncy once saw "a little native man" throw a cricket-ball 119 yards. This is said to beat the English professional record by thirteen yards.

We have all seen the circus-man bound into the air from a spring-board and make a somersault over eight horses standing side by side. Mr. Chauncy saw an aboriginal do it over eleven;

work on the first 10,000 words". (In those days the "type-writer" was the operator, as well as the machine.) Restlessly, Mark Twain continued tinkering with the text and agonizing over the title. He had also secured a competitive offer from another London publisher and, unwilling to negotiate directly with Chatto on such a matter (previously he had used Conway or Osgood), he deputed his friend Bram Stoker, Henry Irving's manager, whose *Dracula* was published the same year, to act for him. Stoker succeeded, and it was to Chatto that the first half of the manuscript was delivered in June.

To speak of the book that resulted from the world tour is misleading, for, contrary to what was long taken for granted, the British *More Tramps Abroad*, as I have demonstrated elsewhere, was not identical with the American *Following the Equator*. Without elaborating excessively on this, *More Tramps Abroad* is roughly half as long again as *Following the Equator* and much less lavishly illustrated, yet each contains some textual matter not in the other. The maxims from Pudd'nhead Wilson's calendar with which each chapter is headed (another and more effective revival of an earlier success) are not always identical, nor are the chapter divisions. The implications of all this are more interesting than the minutiae.

It was the only book Mark Twain ever wrote entirely in England, the only one which Chatto set from the manuscript, where Bliss worked from the typescript. Both survive in the Berg Collection in New York Public Library, and internal evidence indicates how the differences arose. Bliss was less sympathetic to the book than Chatto and deleted large amounts of text, sometimes as not being of interest or readily comprehensible to the American audience, sometimes on more personal grounds. Thus one substantial deletion is accompanied by a note:

A wearisome chapter on aboriginals.
Fr.B.
All dead now.

Sometimes the text is cut simply in order to accommodate illustrations, even if the sense is damaged in the process.

DUNEDIN (*left*), *nineteenth-century watercolour of the New Zealand port, visited by Twain in 1895.*

Chatto, on the other hand, might have been expected to be sensitive to the strongly anti-British thrust of so many chapters in the book and therefore to cut those, but he did not. He wisely reduced the proportion of reprint material from the works of others with which Clemens regularly padded out his travel books, but otherwise Chatto's most significant change results from the marginal query in the manuscript reproduced in my illustration: the sentence is disingenuously modified in the English edition to read "This is said to be within a dozen yards of the professional record".

The only inference from this must be that Chatto had more confidence in the book's marketability than Bliss had. For all his generosity of spirit, Andrew Chatto was a canny enough Scot not to be in publishing as a philanthropist. He usually acted as his own reader, and he was a shrewd judge of a book and of the market. That his home was in Cumberland Terrace, Regents Park, is indicative of his success. It had been written up in 1895 in the same "Celebrities at Home" series in *The World* that, eleven years earlier in happier times, had featured the Clemenses' house in Hartford. The sales figures for this book (again, up to 1907) of 30,000 copies and other evidence in the firm's archives suggest that by the 1890s, despite his international reputation, Mark Twain was a greater commercial asset to his British than to his American publishers.

There is no evidence that Clemens ever realized that the two texts differed. The book and the experiences behind it were so painful to him that he may well never have looked closely at it again once it was on sale and had made its contribution to the set-

ABORIGINEES CALLING "COO-OO-OO-EE" (*left*), *from an engraving, 1863. Twain's American publisher cut from Twain's typescript of* Following the Equator *many passages that he considered would not interest an American readership, including what he called "a wearisome chapter on aboriginals".*

135

VIENNA RINGSTRASSE, *1891 (above). In 1897 Twain went to live for three years in Vienna. It was during this period of self-imposed exile that he finally achieved widespread fame in his own country.*

tling of the debts that he eventually accomplished. Indeed, it was only when he wanted to give Princess Charlotte of Saxe-Meinigen a complimentary copy because of the beauty of the pictures that he realized *More Tramps Abroad* was unillustrated. Chatto did not welcome his suggestion that *Following the Equator* should therefore be imported for sale in Britain.

More Tramps Abroad shows traces of the author's indifference, but it deserves more attention than it receives. As uneven as the earlier travel books, which it resembles in many respects, it differs from them in one significant way: its polemical topicality. Beginning in the usual gossipy, anecdotal fashion, it contains more, and more painstaking, topographical description than its predecessors, and a much greater awareness of the places visited as societies pulsating with human beings and human problems. He is highly censorious of British imperial policy in the Empire, especially of race relations. The kind of chapter Bliss

found wearisome champions the cause of the primitive indigenous inhabitants in a way that does credit to a Southerner who had not been "aware that there was anything wrong" about slavery. What had been implicit in *The Adventures of Huckleberry Finn* becomes explicit in his insistence on the essential humanness of the aborigines, and his indignation at the inhumanity of the cruelty practised on them which he documents vividly and at length.

The borrowings from the writings of others are more judiciously selected, more tellingly deployed, and from more authoritative sources than in the earlier travel books. There is much less humour than in those, much more social criticism, and a genuine, sharp indignation, again well documented, at the disparity between the religiosity of the nineteenth century and the inhuman severity with which it meted out punishment to criminals and the races accepted as inferior. The book is more tightly organized than its predecessors, more of a piece, and is perhaps the nearest Mark Twain comes to producing the serious, topical book for which he wanted to be remembered. Many of the issues that have already been defined as interesting him recur: the Tichborne claimant reappears, and not wholly without relevance; in a museum in Dunedin the spectacle of a lignified caterpillar sets in train a line of anti-Darwinian thought on the suffering inflicted by the process of evolution, and thus on the cruelty of nature; while Huck's "Human beings *can* be awful cruel to one another" might stand as an epigraph to the whole book.

Such humour as there is resides primarily in Pudd'nhead Wilson's maxims, and in many of them, as in those in the original book, there is a homely, Franklinian sardonic wisdom. "Let us be thankful for the fools. But for them the rest of us could not succeed." And Hemingway would have endorsed with enthusiasm the earlier "As to the Adjective, when in doubt, strike it out".

Clemens was so proud of the maxims that he offered to supply Chatto with a new batch every few months for sale as a series of postcards, but this again was not to Chatto's taste.

More Tramps Abroad was Clemens's last major work, though several more volumes of short stories and sketches, such as *The Man that Corrupted Hadleyburg* (1900), appeared. At the end of July 1897 they left Tedworth Square to settle in Vienna and he turned his attention to various minor schemes. He became interested in the celebrated Dreyfus case, and was disappointed at failing to persuade Chatto to commission the book he wanted to write on it. His persistent efforts at becoming a dramatist were continued unsuccessfully with sundry continental collaborators. He sent Chatto, half-seriously, a somewhat bawdy parody of Fitzgerald's *Rubaiyat of Omar Khayyam*, a poem which he genuinely admired. In 1900 he published a wholly serious version of this, shorn of all indelicacy, as a lament at

MARK TWAIN'S SEVENTIETH BIRTHDAY DINNER *(left), held at Delmonico's, New York, on 5 December 1905, was described by the author as "The most satisfying and spirit-exalting honor done me in all my seventy years, oh, by seventy times seventy!". From left to right: Kate Douglas Wiggin, Mark Twain, Joseph H. Twichell, Bliss Carman, Ruth McEmery Stuart, Mary E. Wilkins Freeman, Henry Miles Alden, and Henry H. Rogers.*

THE CATHEDRAL, FLORENCE. *The Clemenses were very fond of this city and Olivia died there in 1904.*

A STERN-STEAMBOAT *(below) of the kind Twain piloted in his youth on the Mississippi River, passes under the Mark Twain Memorial bridge at Hannibal, Missouri.*

the indignities of old age. By now, collected editions of his writings were being published in London and Hartford.

"Man's inhumanity to man" prompted him to various vitriolic shorter protest pieces: *To the Person Sitting in Darkness* (1901) returns to the attack on colonialism. *King Leopold's Soliloquy* (1905) attacks, by pretending to defend, Belgian cruelty to the blacks in the Congo. Clemens was congratulated on this by Arthur Conan Doyle, who shared his views. *The United States of Lyncherdom*, published posthumously, bitterly criticises an outbreak of lynching in Missouri, arguing that American missionaries should return from China to convert the Christians at home. In a similar vein "The War Prayer" (also posthumously published) exposes as hypocritical the conventional prayer for victory which is really a catastrophic infliction of misery, suffering and death on others.

His various anti-vivisection pamphlets recall the fondness for animals that has recurred in his writings ever since *The Jumping Frog*; by now, however, it was acquiring serious overtones in line with his general tendency. In the aphorism "Man is the only animal that blushes – or has reason to", and sometimes bitterly in his blacker satirical pieces, he shows, like Swift before him, "that now and then/Beasts may degenerate into Men". (He would have relished Ezra Pound's similar "Meditatio" on the curious habits of men and dogs.) This sentiment is voiced in *The Mysterious Stranger*, the pessi-

mistic fable to which he devoted so much energy in his closing years. It is a kind of sourly misanthropic inversion of the *Tom Sawyer* theme, in which three young boys in an Austrian hamlet, significantly called Eseldorf ("Ass-village"), are visited by an angel, young Satan (nephew of the original). He demonstrates to them, by various tricks, that the world is run by a malevolent determinism, that the greatest curse of mankind is "the disease called the Moral Sense", and that nothing in human experience is real: it is all a dream. This notion fascinated him, and he continued to explore it, notably in the manuscript he left called "Which Was the Dream?"

What had been aptly called, by Justin Kaplan, "a shrill, philosophically shallow nihilism" dominates most of the work that, in his closing years, he believed would come to be seen as a subversively dangerous gospel. It underlies *The Mysterious Stranger* and was formulated more fully in *What Is Man?* An earlier Mark Twain scholar, Bernard DeVoto, describes it as conveying "the terrible force of an inner cry: Do not blame me, for it was not my fault".

Illness and death dogged his family, and their health became an obsession with him. Ever curious, ever restless, he was lured by any prospect of cures. He became interested in Christian Science, he invested in a high-protein food called Plasmon, in which he had great faith. Then osteopathy attracted him. Disillusioned with Christian Science, he exposed what he saw as its errors in his book on it in 1907. He was forced, of course, to accept mortality.

The family returned to America in 1900, and the last decade of his life was full of popularity, publicity and honours. The University of Missouri gave him an Honorary Doctorate in 1902, en route to receive which he visited Hannibal for the last time. His seventieth birthday in 1905 was another occasion for celebration, and in 1907 he received an Honorary Doctorate of Letters at Oxford. On the same occasion degrees were conferred on the sculptor Rodin, the musician Saint-Saëns and, to his especial pleasure, his old friend Rudyard Kipling. In many ways this was the high point of his career and he missed no opportunity later of wearing his Oxford robes in public, as at the wedding of his daughter Clara in 1909, when his old friend Twichell, the minister, performed the ceremony.

These things were inevitably marred for him by the deaths of his friends and relatives, particularly, of course, by Olivia's. Her terminal illness began in 1902. For long periods he was not allowed even to enter her room; later, when he had taken her back to Florence in the hope that it would help, he was allowed to see her only once a day. Eventually, when she died on 5 June 1904, his grief was accentuated by Clara's succumbing to a nervous breakdown, and for a year he was not allowed to see her either. His other daughter, Jean, developed epilepsy at the same time. The final irony was that trouble developed with his personal secretary, Isabel Lyon, whom he had to dismiss for stealing from him and who conspired with a young Englishman called Ralph Ashcroft, employed as his business secretary, to cheat him. Jean then acted as his secretary, but in 1909 her epilepsy killed her. Clara alone of his family survived him.

In the context of such a catalogue of grief, loneliness and betrayal his confused pessimism ceases to be surprising. Since 1908 they had lived at Stormfield, a house built for him in Redding, Connecticut. Here his main relaxation was his old favourite indoor sport of billiards. He played it with others when he could; he played it alone, except for his memories and his sadness. He developed heart disease ("tobacco heart" he called it, as he dutifully reduced his forty-a-day cigar consumption), paid a visit to Bermuda for the sake of his health, but, deteriorating still, returned to Stormfield where he died on 21 April 1910. No longer could it be said that "the reports of his death were greatly exaggerated". His long love-hate relationship with what he had come to call "the damned human race" was ended, but hundreds of thousands of its members throughout the world mourned the loss of a friend, despite the assertions of the press that his literary reputation was immortal.

Scholarship has perhaps, after all, not served Mark Twain well by assessing his sense of humour too much by modern, sophisticated standards, too little by the popular standards of his day. Dr Johnson's declaration, "I rejoice to concur with the common reader", is a salutary one. Scholarship has also probably placed undue emphasis on the pessimistic determinism unsatisfactorily articulated in the works of Mark Twain's last twenty years, incomplete, unpublished or posthumously issued. It is not being sentimental to focus rather on the tragic spectacle of a lonely, bereaved old man, energetically pouring out words in their thousands, less for communication to others than to clarify for himself the mysteries of his own personality and of an apparently alien universe, with neither of which he could come to terms.

It was Johnson also who defined the function of the author's craft with characteristically sober wisdom: "The only end of writing is to enable man better to enjoy life, or better to endure it." For millions of people throughout the world, Mark Twain, in his own way, has done precisely that. Few can make the same claim.

TWAIN AT THE BILLIARD TABLE, *1905 (above)*.

COLLECTABLES

This aspect of Mark Twain's life and influence has received less attention than might be expected. Bibliophiles and collectors have naturally concentrated on first editions, letters and manuscripts wherever possible; though becoming rarer, and expensive, the supply of these is not necessarily exhausted. Books from Mark Twain's library, I understand, may also still turn up unexpectedly. The pre-1920 English editions of his books can be picked up in secondhand catalogues reasonably inexpensively, as can nineteenth-century piracies (like *Eye-Openers*, reproduced in Chapter 1 of this book).

As these pages suggest, however, there is also a whole field of more ephemeral collectables still to be explored. The authority on these is Mr Nick Karanovich of Fort Wayne, Indiana, and most of these illustrations have been kindly provided by him. Nick Karanovich's wide-ranging collection of books, manuscripts, letters, and other items associated with Mark Twain must be one of the largest still in private ownership. The first exhibition of items from it was mounted in the Lilly Library at Indiana University, Bloomington, in the summer of 1991. The illustrated catalogue of that, and, of course, of other Mark Twain exhi-bitions, could form the basis of an interesting collection in itself. So might postcards of places connected with Mark Twain, postage stamps, programmes of cinema and theatre adaptations of his works, and even the comic book versions that are currently available.

To my knowledge, Mark Twain and his characters did not inspire the kind of plaster or ceramic busts or statuettes that abounded in the case of Dickens. Earlier Americans, notably Washington and Franklin, were the subject of popular Staffordshire figures, but not Mark Twain. Even Royal Doulton, who entered the modern quality market for such figures, include in their large list only Tom Sawyer and Huckleberry Finn, both introduced as late as 1982. Nineteenth-century Staffordshire mugs decorated with Franklin's Poor Richard maxims still survive. Pudd'nhead Wilson does not seem to have prompted similar souvenirs.

The use of Mark Twain's name, image and characters to promote the sale of goods like cigars, tobacco, and even shirts would no doubt have appealed to the business sense of the author who invented a century ago something as modern as Mark Twain's Self-Pasting Scrapbook and whose lively imagination had cast King Arthur's knights in promotional roles.

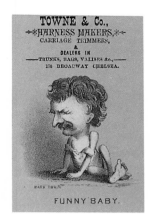

STOCK ADVERTISING CARD (*top, far left*), *c. 1871, for Masseck's Remnant Store, incorrectly gives Twain's real name as "S. H. Clemens". Other imprints with the same image were used for different companies.*

ADVERTISING CARD *for Towne and Co.* (*top centre*), *Harness Makers, of Chelsea, depicting Mark Twain as a "Funny Baby".*

CHINA PLATE (*top left*), *just over nine inches in diameter, imprinted on the reverse with the words "Scammella Trenton China".*

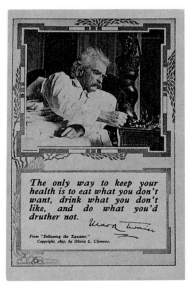

POSTCARD OF THE KITCHEN IN TWAIN'S BOYHOOD HOME (*above*), *the Tom Sawyer House in Hannibal, Missouri, published by the Becky Thatcher Book Shop in Hannibal.*

U.S. POSTAGE STAMP, *1940, (centre row, far left), depicting Mark Twain. One of the Famous American Authors Issue which also included Alcott, Emerson, Cooper and Irving.*

POSTCARD OF MARK TWAIN (*bottom left*), *postmarked "Louisville, KY, December 7, 1912".*

U.S. ADVERTISEMENT FOR PALE ALE *(right), part of a 1991 advertising campaign for Bass Export, using a photograph from the Mark Twain Memorial, Hartford.*

CIGAR-BOX LABEL *(top, far right), chromolithograph describing Mark Twain as "known to everyone, liked by all". His own fondness for cigars was part of his public legend.*

CIGARETTE COUPON *(bottom), with 1885 photograph of a white-suited Mark Twain, for Ogden's Guinea Gold Cigarettes.*

PLAYING CARD *(below), one of sixty-four cards in a game called "Portrait Authors", linking Twain with fellow humorists Josh Billings, Petroleum V. Nasby and the Danbury News Man.*

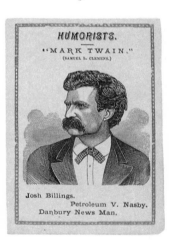

WHAT CAN COMPARE WITH LIFE'S SIMPLE PLEASURES?

Samuel Langhorne Clemens (Mark Twain), 1905.

BASS HELPS YOU GET TO THE BOTTOM OF IT ALL.

© 1991 Guinness Import Company, Stamford, CT.

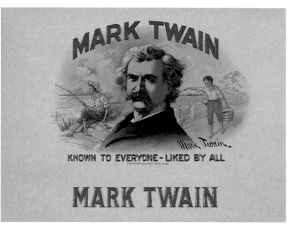

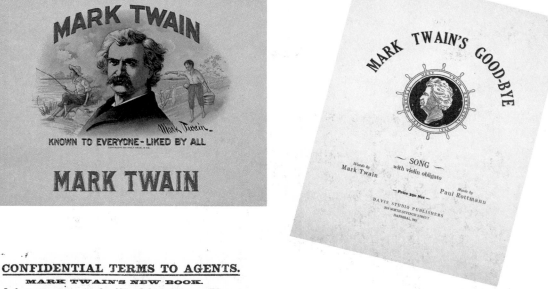

"MARK TWAIN'S GOOD-BYE" *(top left), sheet music for song with words written by Mark Twain, published in Hannibal, Missouri, in 1935 to commemorate the centenary of Twain's birth.*

ADVERTISEMENT FOR CANVASSERS *to sell* Huckleberry Finn *(centre, far left). When the novel was published, Webster acted as a general agent, appointing sub-agents throughout the country.*

SHADOW PICTURE OF MARK TWAIN *(centre, left), one of a set of twenty different pictures incorporated into advertisements dating from 1895 for ladies' scissors.*

GREAT MARK LABEL *(bottom, far left), imprinted on lower edge with the words "Trade Mark registered. 3097 American Label Co. 34–36 Cooper Square N.Y."*

POSTCARD OF THE BECKY THATCHER HOUSE *(below) in Hannibal, Missouri, published by the Becky Thatcher Book Shop. Tom Sawyer's sweetheart Becky was modelled on Laura Hawkins, a school-fellow of Twain.*

INDEX